CU00957003

CONTENTS

INTRODUCTION

Fought between Napoleon's Grande Armée and Austro-Russian forces operating in Moravia, 37 miles (60km) north-east of Vienna and widely regarded as the tactical masterstroke of Napoleon's long military career, Austerlitz stands as one of the greatest victories in military history. A single December day's fighting crushed the Third Coalition, with far-reaching political and strategic implications for French control in Central Europe. Austerlitz also represented a brilliant exercise in grand tactics; in the face of numerically superior forces, Napoleon encouraged Allied commanders to follow the course of action which he intended by establishing a battlefield scenario that he could control, before he proceeded to implement his plan: splitting the Allied army in half before defeating its component parts in turn.

Austerlitz is noteworthy, too, for the fact that Napoleon's prowess and the effectiveness of the Grande Armée as a fighting force reached its apogee there, and it constituted the battle of which the emperor himself was most proud. The climax of a remarkable campaign, Austerlitz crowned the efforts of an army which demonstrated one of the key elements of strategic success: speed. The Grande Armée, poised around Boulogne on the Channel coast for the invasion of England, broke camp and in twenty days reached the Rhine; two months later it entered Vienna;

French bivouac on the evening before Austerlitz. Napoleon's Grande Armée, at the peak of its morale and honed to a superb level of fitness and training between 1803 and 1805, constituted the best fighting force of its generation.

and a fortnight later, under the emperor's command, it destroyed the Third Coalition in an eight-hour engagement. If Napoleon gambled supremely in the campaign of 1805, he generally gambled correctly, partly benefitting from his own well-developed plan, as well as by the errors committed by his opponents.

Austerlitz is all the more remarkable for the fact that it might very well have gone badly wrong. While it began auspiciously when Napoleon's forces enveloped an entire Austrian army at Ulm, in Bavaria, followed by the occupation of Vienna, the Grande Armée faced a potentially perilous position by the following month, for while Austrian forces had been reduced to a remnant, the Russians managed to elude the advancing French and rendezvous with strong reinforcements near Austerlitz. Operating at a considerable distance from France, his resources stretched, facing a coalition mounting operations across a broad front, with the Prussians mobilising sufficient forces to tip the balance against him and with two Austrian armies still intact and situated to his rear, Napoleon could neither retreat for fear of its interpretation as retreat nor pursue the Allies any deeper into Austrian territory lest he risk his own encirclement and destruction. His only option lay in striking quickly and effectively, for he required nothing short of decisive victory.

With this in view, Napoleon sought to entice the Allies into fighting a battle on his own terms – using ground of his choosing and with a strong element of deception – thus compensating for the numerical advantage enjoyed by his opponents. In the event, he did precisely this, selecting an area just west of the village of Austerlitz which offered him the opportunity to design a plan to provoke the Allies into attacking on unfavourable terms. Accordingly, he sent his aide to Allied headquarters, tasked with persuading Tsar Alexander of Russia and Emperor Francis of Austria that Napoleon was anxious to avoid battle and keen to negotiate peace. Napoleon reinforced this impression of timidity by withdrawing his troops from the strategically important

Crossing the River Inn on 28 October, French troops enter Austria. In their strategic plan the Allies certainly never envisaged conducting the campaign on home soil.

The Austrian surrender at Ulm, 20 October 1805, during the campaign in Bavaria prior to the French invasion of Habsburg territory. This and other capitulations left to the Russians responsibility for most of the Allies' next six weeks of campaigning.

Pratzen Heights, west of Austerlitz. By conceding this dominant position to his opponents and by deliberately weakening his right flank, Napoleon encouraged the Allies to attack at points of his designation – all according to his elaborate plan of deception. Finally, in a calculated move, the French emperor positioned his reinforcements well back from view, leaving the impression of weak numbers – and consequently deceived the Allies into seriously underestimating French strength. A strong element of risk attended this plan, however, for success depended entirely on the Allies seizing the heights, and at the same time the French right wing withstanding the onslaught of superior numbers.

Introduction

Quite apart from its significance at the grand tactical level, Austerlitz left a long-standing political legacy, eliminating the last marks of Austrian influence and territorial holdings in Germany and Italy, leaving Napoleon master of half the continent and therefore solidly on the road to establishing the greatest empire in Europe since the fall of Rome – a position achieved only eighteen months after the destruction of the Third Coalition. He consolidated his hold over Italy by annexing the last Habsburg territories in the region, adding them to the Kingdom of Italy, of which Napoleon crowned himself king, and occupied Naples, eliminating the last vestiges of resistance on the peninsula. He placed his sisters on the thrones of several German states, nearly all of which he fashioned into a new political entity: the Confederation of the Rhine, all dependent on, or subservient to, France. On this basis – quite apart from the masterful means employed by Napoleon during the Ulm campaign and at Austerlitz five weeks later – the battle led directly to a substantial shift in the European balance of power, placing France in so dominant a position as to require a further decade of fighting before the Continent could finally eradicate the menace of Napoleonic imperialism.

TIMELINE

1792

20 April	France declares war on Austria, signalling the start of the French Revolutionary Wars
26 June	First Coalition formed between Austria and Prussia, to which Spain, the Holy Roman Empire and other states gradually adhere
20 September	Battle of Valmy; Prussians driven back from their drive on Paris
6 November	Battle of Jemappes, in the Austrian Netherlands (Belgium), as a consequence of which the French occupy Brussels

1793

1 February	France declares war on Britain and the United Provinces (Holland)
7 March	France declares war on Spain
18 March	Battle of Neerwinden
8 September	Battle of Hondschoote

1794

26 June	Battle of Fleurus, Austrian Netherlands

1795

5 April	Treaty of Basle concluded between France and Prussia, the latter of whom leaves the First Coalition
22 July	Spain follows suit, abandoning the First Coalition

Timeline

1796	5 August	Battle of Castiglione; Napoleon's most significant victory thus far of numerous engagements fought in northern Italy against the Austrians since the young general took command on 2 March
1797	14–15 January	Battle of Rivoli; the decisive battle of the Italian campaigns of 1796–97
	17 October	France and Austria conclude peace at Campo Formio, ending the War of the First Coalition and leaving France dominant in the Low Countries, the Rhineland and northern Italy
1799	12 March	War resumes between France and Austria, opening the War of the Second Coalition, which includes Britain, Russia, Turkey and other states
1801	8 February	Peace concluded between France and Austria by the Treaty of Lunéville
1802	25 March	Treaty of Amiens concluded between Britain and France, ending the War of the Second Coalition, from which Russia had already withdrawn in late 1799, as well as the French Revolutionary Wars as a whole
1803	18 May	Renewal of war between Britain and France, inaugurating the beginning of the Napoleonic Wars – a continuation of the Revolutionary Wars on a larger scale rooted largely in a struggle to restore the strategic balance of power in Europe rather than one in pursuit of a monarchical ideological agenda which had played an important role in the previous decade of fighting
1804	18 May	Napoleon proclaimed emperor of the French
	2 December	Napoleon crowned emperor in Notre Dame Cathedral

Austerlitz 1805

11 April	Treaty of Alliance provisionally agreed between Britain and Russia
26 May	Napoleon crowns himself King of Italy
9 August	Austria accedes to the Anglo-Russian alliance, formally establishing the Third Coalition
27 August	Grande Armée leaves camps along the Channel coast and marches for the Danube valley via Bavaria
31 August	Britain and Sweden conclude subsidy agreement for the supply of Swedish troops to the Third Coalition
8 September	Austrian troops enter Bavaria
25 September	Grande Armée reaches the Rhine
3 October	Sweden concludes Treaty of Alliance with Britain, formally joining the Third Coalition
7 October	French main body begins crossing the Danube
11 October	Small body of Austrians surrender at Haslach-Jungingen
13 October	Austrian contingent surrenders at Memmingen
14 October	Battle of Elchingen
14–15 October	Large Austrian cavalry force under Prince Schwarzenberg and Archduke Ferdinand detached from Mack's army to link up with Werneck's corps
15 October	French complete encirclement of Mack
18 October	Murat forces Werneck's capitulation at Trochtelfingen
20 October	Austrian Army under Mack surrenders at Ulm, in Bavaria
21 October	Battle of Trafalgar; Vice Admiral Nelson destroys the Franco-Spanish fleet off Cádiz

Timeline

HISTORICAL
BACKGROUND

A Decade of Bloodshed: The French Revolutionary Wars, 1792–1802

When hostilities broke out in May 1803 between Britain and France – after a brief period of peace lasting fourteen months – this renewed conflict marked the beginning of a series of campaigns, some co-ordinated, others not, which eventually involved practically every state in Europe, known as the Napoleonic Wars (1803–15). The first phase, the War of the Third Coalition, an alliance of Britain, Russia, Austria, Sweden and Naples, arose out of Britain's diplomatic initiative and, to a lesser extent, a similar effort on the part of the tsar and his deputy foreign minister, Prince Adam Czartoryski. It was this coalition – the third attempt by the great (and many lesser) powers to limit the growth of French power and influence – whose fate the Battle of Austerlitz sealed in a single day in December 1805.

To understand the genesis of events which led to that seminal event, one must cast back into the previous decade for, to be strictly accurate, the Napoleonic Wars represented merely an extension of the conflict which had begun a decade before, known as the French Revolutionary Wars. During this series of conflicts, most nations formed at some point part of at least one of the two great yet unsuccessful coalitions seeking to curb the growing power of republican France. We must therefore turn to the roles played by the principal European powers in the great struggles of the 1790s, examine the events which concluded hostilities in 1802, consider the factors which contributed to their renewal in May 1803 and, finally, establish the circumstances which led to the formation of the Third Coalition, whose forces Napoleon shattered in the greatest battle of his long and distinguished command.

Russia, under Tsarina Catherine (the Great), took no part in the War of the First Coalition (1792–97). On her death in 1796 the tsarina was succeeded by her son, Paul, who suffered from bouts of mental illness and quixotic behaviour. In 1799, he joined the Second Coalition (1798–1802) as a consequence of the growing French threat to Russian interests in the Mediterranean, especially the occupation of Malta, seized during Napoleon's expedition to Egypt the previous year, as well as the dissolution of the Order of the Knights of St John of Jerusalem, who had ruled the island since 1530. The dispossessed knights sought assistance from Paul, whom they made Grand Master of the Order. The Russians achieved early successes in the field, fighting in Italy and Switzerland, but relations with Austria became strained and Russia withdrew from the war in late 1799. When Paul was assassinated in a palace coup in March 1801, his 23-year-old son, Alexander, succeeded him as tsar. Alexander and his deputy foreign minister, Prince Adam Czartoryski, were to play prominent roles in the formation of the Third Coalition. In the meantime, with the French ousted by the British from Malta in 1800 and Egypt the following year, Alexander did not renew his country's participation in the War of the Second Coalition (consisting of Austria, Russia, Turkey, Britain, Naples and Portugal). Russia and France concluded a formal peace settlement in October 1801, whereby the French recognised Russia's interests in the eastern Mediterranean and promised to consult Alexander concerning the reorganisation of the borders of many of the small German states, in whose affairs Russia took a great interest, partly as a consequence of the tsar's connection, through his wife, with the Electorate of Baden.

Prussia had, along with Austria, numbered among the first of the Great Powers to declare war on revolutionary France in 1792 and constituted a mainstay of the First Coalition, which would grow to include Spain, Holland, Britain, Sardinia, Naples, Portugal, the minor German states of the Holy Roman Empire and others. She briefly invaded France in 1792, but after her repulse at the Battle of Valmy she ceased to play a significant further part in the war and eventually withdrew from the coalition by the Treaty of Basle in April 1795. Prussia was swiftly followed by Spain, largely owing to the distractions arising to the former, Russia and Austria by the partitions of Poland in 1793 and 1795. Prussia remained neutral during the War of the Second Coalition, though King Frederick William III and Alexander developed a friendship from June 1802, owing to shared interests in limiting French influence in Germany.

Austria, under the Habsburg emperor Francis II, who came to the throne in 1792, controlled a vast Central and Eastern European empire containing a multitude of nationalities,

Emperor Francis II of Austria (1768–1835; reigned from 1792). A determined opponent of Revolutionary and Napoleonic France, he presided over a sprawling, multinational empire which ceded territory as a result of four different punitive treaties, in 1797, 1801, 1805 and 1809.

including Germans, Hungarians, Czechs, Slovaks, Slovenes, Italians, Poles and others, and would prove one of the most implacable enemies of France. Austria remained active throughout the War of the First Coalition, even when practically all the other members, apart from Britain, had abandoned the cause by April 1796. By this point Austria had waged numerous campaigns in the Low Countries and along the Rhine, and was imminently to engage the French in northern Italy under the young General Napoleon Bonaparte. In the event, Bonaparte's campaigns of 1796–97 proved a great success and brought his army within 80 miles (129 km) of Vienna after the decisive French victory at Rivoli, resulting in the Treaty of Campo Formio in October 1797. By its terms, Austria recognised the French occupation of the Austrian Netherlands (Belgium) – overrun by republican forces two years before; conceded the loss of Lombardy; accepted as a *fait accompli* the French occupation of the left bank of the Rhine; and recognised the Cisalpine Republic, a satellite state of the French republic in Italy. Austria, in turn, received territory along the Adriatic coast, Friol and possessions formerly belonging to Venice east of the river Adige. In short, Campo Formio represented a major blow to Habsburg power and prestige.

When the Second Coalition was formed and the campaign began in March 1799, Austria again played the dominant role, with Russia, as briefly described earlier, in support; but the Austrians felt legitimate concern at Paul's erratic behaviour, jealousies persisted over the relative gains resulting from the partitions of Poland and Vienna baulked at the slow speed of Russian forces as they moved west to aid the Austrians in Bavaria and Italy. Both sides met with initial success in these two theatres of operation; however, relations broke down during the subsequent campaign in Switzerland, resulting in the withdrawal of Russia from the war.

Allied fortunes took a further turn for the worse when, in a dramatic move, Bonaparte returned from Egypt, leaving the army behind, and staged a coup in November 1799, resulting

The young General Napoleon Bonaparte at the Battle of Rivoli. The Italian campaigns of 1796–97 established his reputation as a remarkable field commander.

in his rise to power as First Consul. With Austria isolated on the Continent, France renewed the war effort, meeting success in Germany and, despite initial reverses in Italy, Bonaparte began a new campaign in that theatre, leading his army across the Alps in May 1800, capturing Milan and inflicting a serious defeat on the Austrians at Marengo on 14 June. An armistice resulted, but when negotiations failed, the Austrians renewed the campaign and lost decisively at Hohenlinden, near Munich, in December. This resulted in the virtual death blow of the Second Coalition due to the signature of the Treaty of Lunéville in February 1801. By its punitive terms, Austria reaffirmed its commitment to the clauses contained in Campo Formio, which had marked the end of the War of the First Coalition. By signing a separate peace, Austria left Britain as the only major power still opposing France, placing the government under Henry Addington in an awkward diplomatic position, under considerable pressure domestically to make peace.

Historical Background

In the course of Britain's war against revolutionary France between 1793 and 1802, the prevention of French territorial expansion and the re-establishment of the balance of power on the Continent had formed the dominant themes of William Pitt's foreign policy. Principally a naval power, Britain found herself unable to challenge French aggression unassisted. As in the wars against Louis XIV and the various struggles of the mid-eighteenth century, she sought to achieve her war aims through the construction of coalitions with the Great Powers of Europe, including subsidies to support their armies, the seizure of French overseas colonies, harassment of maritime trade and the dispatch of small expeditionary operations to the Continent and the West Indies. Britain also sent armies to the Low Countries in 1793–95, to Holland in 1799 and to Egypt in 1801. The Royal Navy, on the other hand, stood in much greater prominence than the army, fighting several fleet actions – the First of June (1794), Camperdown (1797), St Vincent (1797) and the Nile (1798) – while also engaging in numerous smaller operations in the Atlantic, the Channel, the North Sea and the Mediterranean.

William Pitt (the Younger), prime minister of Britain, 1783–1801 and 1804–06. He played a pivotal role in the construction of the Third Coalition, but died in January 1806 from the cumulative effects of overwork and heavy drinking, a process exacerbated by news of the Allies' defeat at Austerlitz, which left him deeply disconsolate.

Yet such policies – military, naval, financial and diplomatic – consistently failed to cow the power of France, and as we have seen, the fate of the First and Second Coalitions proved a bitter testament to the fact. Poor Allied military co-ordination, mutual jealousies over the territorial spoils of war, ill-conceived strategy and the distractions caused by the partitions of Poland led to the defection of some powers and the defeat of others. At sea, Britain established undisputed command of the waves and conquered virtually the entire French colonial empire, yet proved unable to compensate for the continental advantages reaped by the revolutionary armies in the Low Countries, Germany, Switzerland and northern Italy. Still, France, wearied by wars spawned by revolution and fuelled by her own success, nevertheless desired peace, sending an overture of peace to King George III in March 1801. So long as Britain remained supreme at sea, Napoleon was unable to re-establish the French New World Empire. By virtue of distance, the recent acquisition of Louisiana from Spain could not be exploited, nor could France hope to recover San Domingue (Haiti) from the native rebels who had recently liberated it. With her overseas trade severely curtailed by British blockade and fleet action, France found she could no longer reap the benefits which war on the Continent had provided since 1792; finally, the death of Tsar Paul and his replacement by the more belligerent Alexander, as well as British successes in Egypt in 1801, signalled the end of any prospect of Franco-Russian co-operation against the last remaining members of the Second Coalition: Turkey and Britain.

In Britain, calls for peace were equally pressing. By 1801 the country found itself without continental allies as a result of the series of separate arrangements described earlier between France and Austria, Russia and Prussia, respectively, in the course of the Wars of the First and Second Coalitions. Various states, large and small, had, in fact, begun to turn against Britain's maritime policies of blockade and the principles which underpinned the practice of searching and seizing neutral vessels. No longer would they tolerate Britain's policy of exhorting the Continent to arms, accruing to herself the advantages of colonial acquisitions and overseas markets without the losses attendant upon direct operations against France. In short, while the continental powers stood to lose vast stretches of territory by confronting the republic on land, Britain remained relatively secure from attack. Moreover, little remained in terms of spoils for Britain, for few French colonies still resisted capture, while many of the most important ports of the Continent remained closed to British trade in any event; others that were still open to them, such as those of Portugal, stood on the verge of seizure by hostile Spain. Thus, with Britain mistress of the seas and France supreme on land, both sides regarded further recourse to arms as futile. Protracted negotiations ended the stalemate, and, by the terms of the Treaty of Amiens, concluded in March 1802, an uneasy peace settled over Europe after a decade of uninterrupted war.

The Breakdown of Anglo-French Accord

Just as the origins of the Second World War may be traced back to the Treaty of Versailles of 1919, the origins of the Napoleonic Wars – and specifically the campaign which concluded with the Battle of Austerlitz – may be found in the circumstances surrounding the breakdown of the peace of Amiens. This settlement numbers, like Versailles, among the most controversial ever reached by a British government, for many contemporaries believed Britain had come out considerably worse in the arrangements. This view is largely borne out by an examination of the treaty's terms. The key elements stipulated that all French and Dutch overseas colonies, including the Cape Colony at the southern end of Africa, were to be restored by Britain, whose troops were to evacuate Egypt. France was to receive Elba, while Minorca and Malta were to be returned to Spain and the Knights of St John, respectively. France, for its part, agreed to evacuate the Kingdom of Naples and the Papal States.

Britain's extensive cessions caused alarm and despondency among Pitt and his supporters, who had only recently left office; with seemingly daily evidence to confirm Napoleon's aggressive tendencies, those sacrifices were being keenly felt. The surrender of strategic points around the globe prompted stinging criticism from Lord Grenville and William Windham, the former Secretaries of State for Foreign Affairs and of War and the Colonies, respectively. To such men, the return of all French colonial possessions, along with the return of the Cape Colony and Malta – whose superb port of Valetta served as the Royal Navy's vital strategic base in the central Mediterranean – constituted an act of weakness and humiliation. Nevertheless, the prevailing view in Britain held that the war-weary nation required the respite offered by peace. From the government's perspective, disadvantageous as the terms might be, Britain stood in no position to demand extensive indemnities from France. In the end, however, Amiens offered Britain virtually no security – only a short-lived and costly truce.

The absence of Britain as a signatory to the Treaty of Lunéville, concluded between France and Austria in 1801, had far-reaching consequences, most notably the great potential offered to France for territorial acquisitions on the Continent without the legal interference of Britain. Napoleon was not required to evacuate his troops from Dutch territory or recognise the Batavian Republic's independence; therefore Holland itself, as well as the Cape of Good Hope, a Dutch possession, lay subject to his influence. Nor did arrangements a year later, at Amiens, require French recognition of the sovereignty of the Helvetic (Swiss), Cisalpine (northern Italian) or Ligurian (Genoese) republics, whose independence Lunéville exclusively guaranteed. Consequently, with Austria cowed and exhausted by its defeat in numerous disastrous campaigns stretching back to 1792, the terms of Lunéville could be respected or violated at the First Consul's will, and it is not surprising that contemporary opinion regarded France as the major beneficiary of Amiens. George III himself referred to the peace as 'experimental' – forced on Britain by the abandonment of her allies. It was not long before France reaped the advantages offered at Lunéville and Amiens, for rather than assuage Napoleon's appetite for territorial aggrandisement, Amiens encouraged it; indeed, parallels with the policy of appeasement in the 1930s are not entirely out of place here.

The causes of the rupture of peace are both varied and complex. Britain's mounting discontent with the situation after the signature of the treaty and, ultimately, the country's desire for war rested on three factors: the economic isolation caused by the closure of continental ports to its exports; the encroachment of France on its weak neighbours; and the assembly of military and naval forces along the Channel coast, which Britain interpreted as preparations for invasion.

References to commercial relations were not included in the terms of Amiens. The war had provided Britain with a virtual monopoly over French overseas markets and stimulated commerce with its own colonies. The restitution of enemy colonies ended French dependence on British goods, thus severely damaging those exporters and manufacturers whose livelihoods depended largely on the French market. French control of virtually the entire European coastline from the Scheldt to the Adriatic, and the imposition of heavy customs duties on British goods, all but expelled those goods from continental markets. The renewal of peace also permitted the legitimate pursuit of overseas markets by France without British interference. The extent to which these circumstances may have aroused warlike sentiments on the part of London commercial interests is difficult to assess; however, that they served as an inducement to war there seems little doubt. Since the peace France had, moreover, embarked upon a large shipbuilding programme, ostensibly in support of operations against the rebellious West Indian colony of San Domingue (Haiti), that would in a few years make its navy large enough to challenge Britain's mastery of the seas.

Above all, French continental aggrandisement constituted the chief cause of the renewal of war. French territorial acquisitions during the interlude of peace were extensive. In Italy, Napoleon proclaimed himself president of the Cisalpine Republic in early 1802 and formally annexed Piedmont, and later Parma, in September of that year. Spain ceded Elba to France in August, and French troops reoccupied Switzerland in October – having only evacuated it a few months before – on the pretext of serving a mediating role in internal disputes over the form of government under which the Swiss wished to be ruled. The terms of Lunéville had guaranteed the Swiss the right of self-determination, but Amiens did not. In Britain the reaction was fierce, even to the point that some Whigs, normally sympathetic to peace with France, expressed outrage at the interference with Switzerland's right to self-determination. For the present, at least, British diplomatic language on the affair remained dignified, firm and restrained, demonstrating that Anglo-French relations had not collapsed irreparably. The foreign secretary, Lord Hawkesbury, reminded the French ambassador in London that Napoleon's declared intention,

Charles James Fox, one of the most prominent British politicians of his age, addresses Parliament on the question of the French invasion of Switzerland in 1802.

published in the official government paper *Le Moniteur*, to mediate in the civil disputes in Switzerland violated the pledge to uphold Swiss independence made at Lunéville. France, in short, was to keep its nose out of Swiss affairs. The Swiss gave way to French pressure, and when troops arrived, the small republic made no appeal to arms.

French encroachments were not limited to Central Europe. On 9 October, the Dutch government of the Batavian Republic was informed by the French representative at The Hague that a revolutionary movement was active in Holland and threatening its constitution. In consequence, the First Consul felt it his duty to come to the country's assistance. By the end of the month, Napoleon resolved, in violation of Lunéville, to retain his 10,000 troops of occupation and continued his demand that the republic provide for the maintenance of those forces. The Dutch voiced their objections through their ambassador in Paris, but to no avail. No resistance was offered; disregarding the Dutch rejection of a constitution inspired by himself, Napoleon ordered its forcible imposition.

Thus, in the brief period between March 1802 and May 1803, France came to dominate Holland, Switzerland and north and central Italy without provoking the intervention of the Great Powers. Significantly, these acquisitions did not constitute infractions – in either spirit or letter – of the Treaty of Amiens, only of Lunéville, and therefore Britain's presumptions that the terms of the latter would be fulfilled led them to leave them out of Amiens; as such, their objections could find no foundation in international law. Thus, by the autumn of 1802, barely six months after the signature of the treaty, Britain already stood on the brink of going to war.

Anglo-French relations now deteriorated rapidly. As a result of French depredations on the Continent, Addington soon resolved not to act on his pledge to withdraw British troops from Malta, thus preserving some point of strategic value from which to check, if necessary, French encroachments into the Mediterranean. Malta's importance had long been recognised by the European powers. It had been occupied by Bonaparte in 1798 while en route to seize Egypt and retaken after a two-year siege by British troops on land and blockade by a squadron of the Royal Navy at sea. Although British diplomats made great efforts at the peace conference to secure the island's annexation, Bonaparte steadfastly refused to accept this provision and instead proposed its neutrality under the guarantee of a third party: the weak Kingdom of Naples. Britain considered the establishment of a Neapolitan garrison, to deter future French designs on Malta, a ridiculous proposition; pending the accession of the other Great Powers to an article guaranteeing the island's independence, later known as Article X, Britain ultimately acquiesced to the condition. Nonetheless, she was remiss in failing to evacuate the island and admit the 2,000 men of the Neapolitan garrison within the three-month period allowed after the signature of the treaty, and, moreover, failed to withdraw entirely its garrison from Egypt, where a portion of its troops had remained in Alexandria since the country's restoration to Turkey. It was not until the First Consul issued a demand for its complete withdrawal that Britain satisfied the conditions of the treaty on this point.

Austria had already acceded to the article guaranteeing the sovereignty and independence of Malta, and Russia, despite the conditional nature of its acceptance, was thought to be amenable to accession. In London, however, the prime minister contemplated retaining the island. Addington's continued delay in removing British troops soon amounted to an overt violation of the treaty; France was not prepared to let this pass unnoticed, and on 27 February Talleyrand reminded Lord Whitworth of Britain's solemn obligations. Only the accession of Russia to Article X and the election of a new Grand Master of the Order of Malta were wanting, the French foreign minister stated. Thus, the time for delay afforded by a pretext for continued occupation would soon come to an end.

Although Britain had originally agreed to Malta's evacuation in good faith, in light of French depredations on the Continent since the signature of Amiens, Addington balked at relinquishing the island to an uncertain fate under a Neapolitan garrison, notwithstanding pledges from Russia, Prussia, Austria and other powers to guarantee the island's independence. Moreover, various reports from British envoys, including Sir John Warren at St Petersburg and the Earl of Elgin, former ambassador to Turkey, aroused suspicions at Downing Street that France was contemplating a renewal of its previous designs on Turkey. If these reports alone did not convince the Cabinet to retain the garrison indefinitely, a report published in *Le Moniteur* in January 1803 reconfirmed Addington's conviction that Malta's evacuation would be catastrophic to British interests in the Mediterranean in general, to Egypt specifically and, by extension, to India. Similarly, it reinforced prevailing views within British political and public circles of Bonaparte's boundless ambitions.

The report was the product of the mission of Colonel Horace Sebastiani, a French infantry (later cavalry) officer temporarily charged as an envoy to Turkey. Sebastiani undertook extensive travels in Egypt, the Levant and the Balkans ostensibly to acquire commercial information on these regions. Irrespective of its true purpose, the mission yielded valuable intelligence on the state of defence of various Ottoman provinces for purposes of future French conquest. The publication of Sebastiani's report, in which, among other conclusions, he observed that 6,000 troops could easily subdue Egypt, excited indignation in Britain and resolved Addington to refuse the evacuation of Malta as agreed to at Amiens.

In early February, Lord Whitworth, the British ambassador in Paris, informed the French government that Malta would be retained in compensation for the extensive territorial gains acquired by France since the signature of Amiens – although British troops did leave the Cape of Good Hope, captured in 1795 from the Dutch, in accordance with Amiens, that month. These gains had completely overturned the balance and stability that both powers had pledged to uphold. As the state of possession had been so radically altered, Britain reserved the right, the government argued, to seek compensation on the basis of diplomatic precedence in international law and the assumed sanction of this principle by France. In view of French gains in Holland, Switzerland and Italy, the British government believed it consistent with the terms of Amiens to claim for itself compensation in order to balance the threat to its security which these colonial acquisitions represented; in short, Britain

Lord Whitworth, British ambassador in Paris, conducting talks with the First Consul during the opening months of 1803. Anglo-French relations soured over such issues as the British refusal to evacuate its garrison from Malta and the equally strident refusal by France to withdraw its troops from Switzerland and Holland.

demanded a counterweight to French gains. The Sebastiani report, moreover, suggested continued French designs on Egypt – a wholly unacceptable prospect in British eyes. Whitworth recapitulated these arguments to the foreign minister in mid-February. Talleyrand assured him that France entertained no designs on Egypt or India and referred to Sebastiani's mission as a strictly commercial venture. The First Consul, he continued, had no desire to disturb the peace reached at Amiens, and claimed that French finances would not, in any event, enable him to wage war. Finally, he expressed surprise that the British government should hold any suspicion of French intentions.

Within days, Napoleon summoned Whitworth to the Tuileries to explain his position in person. The First Consul enumerated the various provocations for which he held Britain accountable and referred particularly to its failure to evacuate Malta and Egypt in accordance with Amiens. France, he declared, could not tolerate British possession of Malta. He complained about the virulent personal attacks against him in the British press and accused Britain of harbouring French émigrés who, he claimed, had conspired to overthrow his government. If he had intended to invade Egypt, the First Consul informed Whitworth, it would already have been accomplished. Napoleon claimed that he would not conquer Egypt, much as he would like it as a colony, since he could obtain it without recourse to war as a result of the inevitable collapse and dismemberment of the Ottoman Empire, or by some private arrangement with the sultan.

On the strength of such words, it was clear in Britain by the first months of 1803 that the conduct of France could no longer be tolerated, and many politicians, both within the government and on the opposition benches in Parliament, were either calling for war or held the view that it was only a matter of time before events forced Addington's hand and made hostilities unavoidable. Bonaparte's expressed view to the *Corps Législatif* in February that the nation's defence required the raising of 480,000 troops only strengthened this view. With Anglo-French relations thus rapidly deteriorating, war looming on the horizon and naval preparations actively under way in French and Dutch ports, on 6 March Addington directed the Cabinet to sit and consider the defence of the nation. By the end of the month, measures were in hand to strengthen British defences in the West Indies, new naval commanders were assigned to stations operating in home waters and Parliament voted to embody the militia and increase the navy by 10,000 men.

For its part, France rightly accused Britain of delinquency in evacuating Malta which, as noted earlier, was by the terms of Amiens meant to be returned to the Knights of St John. Though Britain was prepared to evacuate the island as soon as a new Grand Master of the Order was elected and the Great Powers agreed to guarantee the island's independence, neither of these conditions was ever fulfilled, principally owing to the renewal of war. In any event, there was reason to believe that the Knights of St John and the Neapolitan envoy at Malta were colluding with French officials. The island therefore continued firmly under British occupation, and after numerous abortive attempts by Whitworth to settle the Malta question, the ambassador left Paris. His departure heralded nothing unexpected in Britain, for by May 1803 repeated French provocations had, for many, long justified a declaration of war. In support of his belligerent policy, Addington laid before Parliament a large collection of Foreign Office dispatches that concerned the course of negotiations with France since Amiens, as well as supplementary materials equally damning of the First Consul. Many in Parliament, and in the nation at large, believed circumstances vindicated Britain's cause, and on 18 May the House of Commons voted its approval for a declaration of war on France.

The decision was grimly taken, for although some observers expressed hopelessly optimistic views on the nation's prospects of success, the fact remained that Britain embarked on a war without a single ally. Moreover, if the 'Amiens interlude' had clearly enabled Napoleon to aggrandise power at the expense of his weaker neighbours, with hostilities resumed with Britain he stood all the better placed to capitalise on circumstances. Thus, on 1 June a large French force assembled in Holland invaded the Electorate of Hanover, the hereditary protectorate of King George III, enabling the French to exclude British commerce from much of the north-west German coast and provoking Britain to retaliate with a naval blockade of the French coast. In the Mediterranean, French troops occupied the remainder of the Italian peninsula apart from a portion of the Kingdom of Naples, which remained under constant menace. Britain's greatest concern, however, focused on the concentration of French forces at Boulogne, massing for an invasion of the south coast of England – a process which entailed an increase in naval production, backed by an army of 160,000 men. A massive industry of flat-bottomed barges flourished in northern Europe to support the projected Channel crossing.

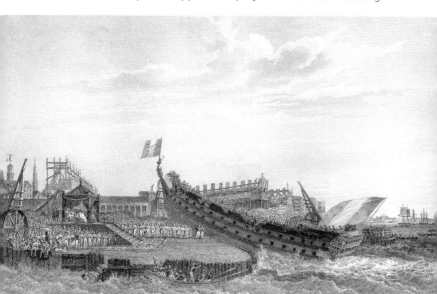

Launching of an eighty-gun ship of the line at the port of Antwerp.
The accelerated naval construction programme raised justifiable fears in
Britain about French intentions to invade.

To counter this, the army in the British Isles numbered only 90,000, but a further 80,000 men could be drawn upon in the militia, and 400,000 civilians joined the vast array of volunteer units. About a quarter of the volunteers, however, trained with pikes instead of muskets owing to a shortage of firearms. The mainstay of the country's defence rested with the Royal Navy, whose Channel Fleet stood in the first line, while ships blockaded Brest, Cherbourg, Toulon and the other major French ports to bottle up the opposing fleets.

The Formation of the Third Coalition, 1803–05

The rupture of the peace of Amiens fourteen months after its signature ushered in a new era of conflict, which soon assumed global proportions and was to span another twelve years. The two great rivals pitted their energy and resources against one another in a struggle to decide between French continental hegemony and the restoration of the balance of power. Yet Britain well

'PITT'S GOLD'

As part of his propaganda campaign to sow the seeds of Allied disunity and play upon natural Anglophobia within France, Napoleon often portrayed Britain as the cynical paymaster of the Third Coalition, using 'Pitt's gold' to subsidise continental armies and thereby relying on them to bear the brunt of the fighting while the British Army undertook only minor expeditionary operations at little expense in blood. The fact remained that Britain's modestly sized army precluded her from involvement in major ground operations – though the Royal Navy carried out the important function of clearing the seas of French merchant vessels and blockading French ports. Moreover, Britain's financial clout enabled her to offer £5 million for Austria and Russia to field up to 400,000 troops, plus another £1.25 million if Prussia joined the coalition with 100,000 men.

understood that this could never be achieved unilaterally, and thus assumed her traditional role as the architect of coalitions.

Initially, this enterprise proved frustrating and fruitless, for though Russia appeared a viable partner for an alliance with Britain, the prospect of co-operation from the other two Great Powers, Austria and Prussia, remained considerably more distant. The Habsburg monarchy, its treasury empty, was only just recovering from the French Revolutionary Wars, while Prussia continued to maintain the policy of neutrality that she had adopted since leaving the First Coalition in 1795 – notwithstanding her objections to the French occupation of Hanover, which she herself had long coveted in a bid to increase Prussian power in north Germany.

Russia, therefore, represented Britain's greatest hope as a prospective ally. After concluding peace with France in October 1801, Alexander found himself snubbed on a number of occasions, beginning with the territorial settlements involving the minor German states in 1802–03, in which Napoleon only involved Russia insofar as it contributed to encouraging Austria to acquiesce to territorial losses to German princes, whom Napoleon sought to woo into his sphere of influence. Moreover, Napoleon declined to recognise Alexander's desire to protect the interests of Sardinia; the tsar's objections to the occupation of Switzerland also went unheeded. France had stood some chance of thwarting a possible Anglo-Russian accord in light of the friction caused between London and St Petersburg over the question of a garrison for Malta, but Napoleon failed to profit from these disagreements when, by early 1803, the Sebastiani report and other intelligence on French intentions in the Near East, Egypt, the Levant and Greece raised Russian suspicions over French designs involving wide swathes of territory bordering the Mediterranean. The tsar grew uneasier still when the French occupied Piedmont and Parma, which led Alexander to back Britain's unilateral retention of Malta.

On the other hand, Alexander maintained that Britain's refusal to evacuate Malta had strongly contributed to the outbreak of war in the first place, and Franco-Russian relations as war began stood on a civil footing – enough for Napoleon, in June, to request that Alexander serve as a mediator between France and Britain. Alexander, keen to play a more active role in European affairs, accepted the offer; but when he presented proposals in July, which satisfied neither party and led to talks collapsing the following month, Franco-Russian relations soured. They were further worsened by Napoleon's public tirade on 25 September against the Russian ambassador in Paris, Count Markov, whom the tsar, outraged by this snub, recalled to St Petersburg.

Alexander's gradual orientation towards Britain received impetus from Prince Adam Czartoryski, his deputy foreign minister, amongst other advisers. Alongside growing concern over increasing French activity in the Balkans, the Adriatic and in Turkey, in November discussions with Britain on the possibility of forming an alliance began in earnest. Still, Russia was reluctant to do so without the aid of both Austria and Prussia, neither of which would come forth. Sweden, on the other hand, though economically and militarily weak, in December enthusiastically offered to join Britain, with King Gustavus IV anxious not only to destroy French 'Jacobinism' as a threat to royalism across Europe, but with a particular view to protect his north German possession of Pomerania.

Threats posed by royalist conspirators against Napoleon contributed strongly to the impetus behind the formation of the Third Coalition, by inadvertently provoking the French government into violating international law. The first attempt on the First Consul's life in 1800 had failed, but London served as a base for a coterie of conspirators, most notably George Cadoudal, a leader of the royalist movement in the Vendée, and Jean-Charles Pichegru, a former revolutionary general who wished to restore the Bourbon monarchy. The British government financially supported these and other plotters as part of a larger network of royalist agents extending across the Continent, but particularly within France itself.

Napoleon's spies managed to penetrate the movement, in so doing discovering that a Bourbon French prince numbered amongst the conspirators, who planned to land an armed émigré force on the French coast. Police arrested Pichegru, Cadoudal and others working clandestinely in Paris, in February and March 1804. When information gleaned from the suspects' papers indicated that the duc d'Enghien, a royalist émigré of the Condé line of the Bourbon family, lay behind a plan for a royalist landing, Napoleon dispatched troops to Ettenheim, just over the French border in neutral Baden, to apprehend the prince and bring him to Paris. Cavalry surrounded the house on the night of 14/15 March and seized the prince at dawn, together with his papers, and conveyed him to the Chateau de Vincennes. There, on 20 March, at a hastily convened court martial which denied the prisoner the benefit of a legal defence, the duke admitted an intention to command troops against the French republic and of receiving funds from the British government, but the prosecution failed to find proof of d'Enghien's involvement in Cadoudal's plot to kill the First Consul – the actual charge laid against the accused. The 'court' nevertheless convicted d'Enghien of treason and executed him by firing squad the following day in the dry moat of the fortress. Many émigrés, including Pichegru, implicated in the plot to overthrow Napoleon's government were imprisoned or exiled, but eleven, including Cadoudal, were executed, in his case on 10 June.

The impact on the royal houses of Europe of the execution of the duc d'Enghien cannot be overestimated, for it caused revulsion the extent of which Napoleon could not have anticipated – not least in St Petersburg, where the news gave new impetus to Anglo-Russian accord and, with the return to government of William Pitt, sped the diplomatic efforts of the British government to create a grand coalition involving Russia, Austria, Prussia and other powers. Not only did Alexander condemn the arrest and execution of d'Enghien as a violation of the territorial sovereignty of a neutral power and an act of murder, but he also took particular exception owing to the fact that the Margrave (later Elector) of Baden was his father-in-law. Alexander ordered his court into mourning and sent a note of protest to Paris. The reply insulted

Conference in London between Pitt and envoys sent by the tsar to discuss plans for an Anglo-Russian alliance. The occupation of Malta formed the principal point of contention between the two countries and nearly jeopardised the entire diplomatic initiative.

him deeply, suggesting his complicity in the assassination of his father, Paul, and alluding to the role of British 'gold' in backing the royalist conspiracy. The decision of the French Senate two months later to confer on Napoleon the title 'Emperor of the French', with the coronation to follow in December, only served to aggravate the monarchies of Europe further still.

The d'Enghien affair may be seen as a pivotal event amongst the various elements which drew the belligerents of the Third Coalition together, for from the spring of 1804 Russia redoubled her diplomatic efforts to secure alliances, not only with Britain, who had begun the whole process the previous year, but with Austria, Prussia and Sweden. Specifically, Russia began secret talks with Prussia in May to prevent further French encroachments into Germany and in the following month negotiations between Britain and Russia began to lay down the main features of a coalition to include Austria and Sweden, and hopefully Prussia as well.

Anglo-Russian negotiations entered a more advanced stage in January 1805, when Pitt sent a lengthy state paper to St Petersburg outlining the proposed coalition's war aims and the general strategy to be adopted across various theatres of operation.

In the meantime, Russia and Austria concluded a defensive alliance in November 1804 and an Anglo-Russian alliance was provisionally signed in April 1805, though both sides would wrangle for some months about the Russian demand for Britain to evacuate Malta. Conveniently, Napoleon broke the diplomatic deadlock when he crowned himself King of Italy in Milan on 26 May and proceeded to annex Genoa early the following month. The contentious issues then dividing Anglo-Russian harmony fell by the wayside, and on 28 July an alliance formally came into force, followed by Austria's assent on 9 August. Sweden and Naples would join the coalition shortly thereafter. This left only Prussia to be persuaded or cajoled into co-operation, for Allied success depended heavily on the united efforts of Britain, Russia, Austria and Prussia, at a minimum. Despite, however, the closeness between Alexander and Frederick William, Prussia declined to join the alliance, partly out of fear of France and partly lured into neutrality by the offer of Hanover, seized from Britain in 1803.

THE ARMIES

The French Army

In the summer of 1805 the Grande Armée constituted probably the finest fighting force of the revolutionary and Napoleonic era. It had begun life in 1803 as *L'Armée de l'Angleterre*, with a strength of about 180,000 men camped along the Channel coast from Holland to Brest, but with the bulk concentrated around Boulogne, poised for Napoleon's projected invasion of England. It was with the bulk of these troops, later supplemented by others, that the emperor, in response to the (unexpected) formation of the Third Coalition, altered his plans and marched to the Danube valley.

For the two preceding years the Grande Armée had trained intensively in musketry, marching, formation change and fieldcraft, attaining in the process a high state of proficiency, discipline and morale. Soldiers drilled regularly at platoon, company and battalion level, and though less frequently in exercises involving higher formations such as brigades and divisions, they nevertheless constituted the only force in the War of the Third Coalition which could boast of this capability. Officers at all but the most junior levels possessed a wealth of combat experience, showed themselves highly capable and maintained strong bonds

Emperor Napoleon I (1769–1821)

Born in Corsica, Napoleon received his military education in France and in 1792, at the outset of the Revolutionary Wars, served as an officer in the artillery in the Army of Italy. In 1793, at the siege of Toulon, by suggesting the sighting of guns over the harbour, he played an instrumental part in forcing the Allied fleet to withdraw, leaving the royal inhabitants to their fate. Promoted from captain all the way to brigadier, he was present in Paris in 1795 during a royalist uprising that threatened the government, known as the Directory. In suppressing the riot by sweeping the streets with grapeshot, Napoleon earned the gratitude of the government, who promoted him to *général de division* and gave him command of the Army of Italy – a rag-tag, poorly equipped and trained formation on a subsidiary front. During a remarkable period of leadership between 1796 and 1797, Napoleon managed to raise morale and convert his army into a first-rate fighting force, which knocked the Piedmontese out of the war and drove the Austrians out of northern Italy. Unilaterally assuming a diplomatic role, Napoleon personally laid down the terms of the Treaty of Campo Formio and sent the results to bewildered – yet impressed – government officials in Paris. In 1798 he proposed a plan for an expedition to Egypt as a prelude to an attack on British India. He captured Cairo, but with the destruction of the French fleet at the Battle of the Nile, Admiral Nelson left Napoleon's army isolated. Napoleon succeeded in taking the campaign as far as Acre, on the Syrian coast, but having learned of numerous French setbacks on the Continent at the hands of the Second Coalition and frustrated by limited success in Egypt, he returned to France, albeit after the military crisis had passed. He initiated a *coup d'état* in November 1799 and assumed the dominant position in the new government as First Consul. Renewed war with Austria in 1800 led him to assume command of the army in northern Italy, where he inflicted a serious defeat at Marengo, which strengthened his political situation. He instituted a series of internal social and legal reforms in France, most notably the *Code Napoléon*, and secured his political base permanently by assuming the title of emperor on 2 December 1804, exactly a year before the Battle of Austerlitz.

Austerlitz 1805

Napoleon issuing eagles to his regimental colonels. The eagle, an ornament mounted on reigmental flagstaffs, represented the sacred bond between the soldier and his unit and served as a rallying point on the battlefield.

with their men. The army contained a high proportion of veterans of the Revolutionary Wars, some of whom had fought as recently as the campaign of 1800 at Marengo or Hohenlinden, but many others who had served in one or more of the various campaigns between 1792 and 1801: on the Rhine, along the Pyrenees, in the Low Countries, in Italy, the Vendée, Switzerland, the West Indies, Egypt or Syria – often, several of these. A quarter of the army personnel had served since 1792, while over 40 per cent possessed prior military service, quite apart from the two years' training now under their belts while stationed in France, Holland or Hanover.

The army consisted of seven corps – most of which served at Austerlitz – a self-sustaining, all-arms formation of infantry, cavalry and artillery which could engage independently in combat for as long as a day, but which normally acted in tandem with like formations. Each corps contained two or three divisions, each of two or three brigades of infantry, one of light cavalry, plus a complement of artillery and engineers. Each brigade normally contained two regiments, with these sub-divided into battalions: the basic infantry fighting unit.

Infantry, other than that of the Imperial Guard, were classed as either line (*ligne*) or light (*légère*), their role differing by the fact that line units fought in tight formations – shoulder to shoulder in line or column. In contrast, light infantry could perform these same functions, but usually fought in skirmish order, an extended line with soldiers firing independently rather than by volley for the purposes of harassing an approaching or fleeing enemy, or creating a screen to mask formed units behind them. In 1805 the army numbered nineteen line and four light regiments, comprising four battalions each, and seventy line and twenty-three light regiments composed of three battalions each. Each line battalion consisted of nine companies, with a theoretical strength of 123 officers and men in the seven fusilier companies and the single company of elite *voltigeur* (literally 'vaulters', i.e. light troops organic to the battalion), and ninety-nine officers and men in the single grenadier company. Light infantry battalions contained the same number of companies, though the elite company consisted of carabiniers, with chasseurs serving the ordinary, counterpart role of fusiliers in the line regiments. On paper, therefore, French infantry battalions numbered over 1,000 men, though they seldom approached this in reality. Apart from the line and light regiments, the Grande Armée also contained a Reserve Grenadier Division, under General Nicolas Oudinot, composed entirely of the grenadier companies drawn from the regiments stationed along the Rhine and serving maritime defence duty along the coasts. By converging these subunits, the army produced seventeen provisional grenadier battalions.

The cavalry consisted of light, medium and heavy regiments. Cuirassiers and carabiniers comprised large horses bearing large men fitted with a cuirass – steel breast and back plate, and helmet, and wielding a long, heavy straight sword meant for thrusting. These regiments constituted the 'shock' element of the mounted arm, with the charge their raison d'être. Heavy cavalry regiments were consolidated into separate reserve divisions rather than distributed among the infantry corps. Medium cavalry

Napoleon distributing the Legion d'Honneur *during an inspection of the camp at Boulogne in August 1804.*

consisted of dragoons, who could fight on foot with their carbine, but normally served on horseback, either in separate divisions or as an integral part of an infantry corps. Light cavalry consisted of hussars (ornately dressed units tracing their origins to Hungarian horsemen) and *chasseurs à cheval*, both of whom carried a light, slightly curved sabre either to charge the enemy – usually opposing light cavalry or guns – or more usually to perform such vital functions as exploiting gaps in the enemy line, pursuing fleeing troops, harassing skirmishers or guarding the flanks of friendly infantry formations. French cavalry in 1805 suffered from serious shortages of mounts and thus regiments routinely reached the field understrength. Thus, while all cavalry regiments contained four squadrons of 180 men each for a total theoretical strength of 720 officers and men, units rarely achieved this figure. In all, the cavalry consisted of two regiments of carabiniers, twelve of cuirassiers, thirty of dragoons, twenty-four of *chasseurs à cheval* and ten of hussars. In total, these numbered 312 squadrons, though with shortages of mounts some troopers, particularly the dragoons, had to serve on foot.

The Imperial Guard (*Garde Impériale*) formed the army's elite reserve, composed of veterans of several recent campaigns and led by combat-experienced officers drawn from line units and distinguished for their bravery and loyal service. The Guard infantry consisted of two battalions of *grenadiers à pied*, two of *chasseurs à pied* and one of marines of the guard, each of about 1,500 men. The cavalry included four squadrons each of *chasseurs à cheval* and *grenadiers à cheval*, a company of Mamelukes and two squadrons

Sabres drawn, French cuirassiers await the order to charge.

of elite gendarmes. Like their counterparts in the line, the Guard cavalry seldom mustered their establishment strength.

All told, the French Army and its allies – the latter composed of small contingents from Bavaria, Württemberg, Baden, Holland and Italy – numbered 499 battalions and 354 squadrons, though these were spread across several major formations, including the Army of Italy under Marshal Masséna, the Army of Reserve in France under Joseph Bonaparte, the Army of Naples under Gouvion St Cyr and over 150 battalions deployed along the coasts and in the colonies. This left, for the coming campaign in Bavaria and Moravia, the Grande Armée itself, consisting of 190 battalions and 213 squadrons of cavalry, plus artillery.

The Austrian Army

The forces of the Habsburg monarchy laboured under a number of difficulties in 1805, not least the myriad problems created by the drastic reductions in military spending undertaken in the wake of the disastrous campaign of 1800 in northern Italy and Bavaria. From the following year, Archduke Charles, a younger brother of Emperor Francis and probably the best field commander in the empire, began to introduce widespread reforms in his capacity as Minister of War, including major changes to army administration, only to encounter considerable opposition from entrenched conservative elements within the senior officer corps. They were prepared only to tolerate changes to the structure and regimental-level administration of the army rather than to the higher apparatus which managed and controlled it. Charles managed to overcome some of these obstacles, but other largely intractable problems remained, including the poor pay and standards of education characteristic of those in junior officer rank; incompetence amongst some of their superiors, who owed their positions to noble or otherwise exalted lineage; and the scarcity of opportunities for army exercises on a major scale by virtue of unit dispersion over the vast Habsburg realms. Perhaps worst of all, the decision to appoint General Mack as Chief of Staff in April 1805 resulted in a series of rapid, ill-timed changes which broke down the previous structure by which officers and men knew one another, for by increasing the number of field battalions from 192 to 318 and creating 122 new reserve companies, men of all ranks found themselves shifted into new units or subunits at the worst

Austrian line infantryman and light cavalryman, known as chevauleger. *Such troops were dependable and reasonably well trained, but not the equal of their French counterparts in 1805.*

possible time: on the eve of war. Compounding the problem, this dramatic increase in unit numbers naturally stimulated a corresponding demand for more officers, yet with no realistic possibility of training them in the twelve weeks before the troops left for service in southern Germany and northern Italy.

The rank and file of the Austrian Army represented a wide range of nationalities owing to the disparate ethnic complexion of the empire, with Germans comprising the dominant group, followed by Hungarians – numerous enough to form their own line and grenadier battalions – as well as Italians, Croats, Serbs, Poles, Walloons (from Belgium, a Habsburg possession until 1795) and others. Conscription met most of the recruitment needs of the army, with terms of service ranging from ten years in the infantry to twelve in the cavalry and fourteen in the artillery and engineers. In 1805, by virtue of the very recent organisational changes undertaken just prior to hostilities, all sixty-one line infantry regiments contained four four-company field battalions each: two of fusiliers, one of grenadiers and one depot battalion of fusiliers. Battalions in the field tended to number approximately 500 men each, although official strength stipulated about 800. Apart from the regular infantry, the army maintained seventeen *Grenz* (border) regiments, who normally served in a light infantry role along the wild frontiers with the Ottoman Empire, and of which three battalions of four companies each served in the campaign of 1805. The army also contained Tyrolean militia, and volunteer *jäger* and garrison battalions, though none of these served at Austerlitz itself. According to recent changes in drill introduced by Mack as late as June, infantry would now deploy in two ranks instead of the three employed by practically all other European armies except the British.

Divided into most of the same categories as their counterparts in the French and Russian armies, Austrian cavalry enjoyed a high reputation across Europe. Six regiments of *chevauxlegers* (light horse), twelve of hussars and three of *uhlans* (lancers) served in the light role associated with reconnaissance, patrolling and guarding flanks, though all of these were capable of executing the charge. Six regiments of dragoons performed a multi-functional role as in other armies, and eight regiments of cuirassiers, again as elsewhere, provided the real punching power of the mounted arm. All regiments, irrespective of class, contained eight squadrons, for a theoretical strength of just over 1,000 officers and troopers, though in the field the acute shortage of horses rendered this figure illusory. The Austrian Army was also noted for its high standard of artillery, but savage cuts in recent years deprived this service of adequate manpower, equipment and draught horses for pulling the guns and ammunition *caissons*.

Austrian cuirassier and dragoon, representing heavy and medium cavalry, respectively. The former wore a black cuirass or breastplate, which could deflect the cut and thrust of a sword but could not stop a musket ball.

In the campaign of 1805, Habsburg forces served on numerous fronts with varying strengths: the Army of Italy, under Archduke Charles, contained 171 battalions of infantry and 96 squadrons of cavalry; the Army of Germany, under Archduke Ferdinand, with Mack as chief of staff and de facto commander, comprised 88 battalions and 148 squadrons, later to be reinforced by substantial Russian forces under General Mikhail Kutuzov; and the Army of the Tyrol, under Archduke John, consisted of 65 battalions and 16 squadrons. All the aforementioned formations contained a complement of artillery and engineers. Finally, numerous reserve units served in garrisons across the empire, especially in Hungary, thus releasing regular troops for active operations.

The Russian Army

Tsar Alexander's forces in 1805 represented the product of recent reforms undertaken since the death of his father, Paul, four years earlier. During his short reign, Paul had quixotically dressed and drilled his soldiers in an outdated, anachronistic manner reminiscent of the days of Frederick the Great of Prussia, with uniforms of mid-eighteenth-century inspiration chosen for their impressive appearance rather than practicality or comfort. The new reforms also swept away the radical changes to internal organisation recently undertaken by Count Arakcheev, during whose tenure in the War Ministry the number of infantry battalions rose and fell in an illogical and disruptive fashion, a situation worsened by his decision to substitute traditional regimental titles with the personal names of their respective unit commanders.

Still, much remained as before: most soldiers continued to enter the army according to an annual levy which required twenty-five years' service of these impoverished souls, the overwhelming majority of whom comprised serfs accustomed to hard, spartan lives on the edge of subsistence. They thus formed the basis for a group of tough, obedient soldiers capable of enduring with little complaint even the severest of hardships on campaign. The

Prince Peter Ivanovich Bagration (1765–1812)

Born in Georgia, Bagration joined the Russian Army in 1782, thereafter serving in the Caucasus in 1783–86 and 1790, and against the Turks in 1788. He was posted to a cavalry regiment in Poland in 1794 and, under Suvorov's wing, became a general major in 1799, during which year he led the Advance Guard in Italy and, later, the rear guard in Switzerland. During the Austerlitz campaign he commanded the 1st Column of Kutuzov's army, and earned a reputation as one of the most competent generals the Russians put into the field. Few Allied officers escaped from the disaster of 1805 with their reputations entirely intact, but Bagration earned promotion to general lieutenant during its course, and unlike a number of his colleagues, including Kutuzov, he would serve in the campaign of 1806–07 in Poland against the French. He contributed strongly to the campaign of 1808 against Sweden during the Russian invasion of Finland and was commander-in-chief of the Army of Moldavia in the campaign of 1809 in the war against Turkey (1806–12). When the French invaded Russia in 1812, Bagration commanded the Second Army of the West, but died in September as a result of wounds received at Borodino.

RUSSIAN INFANTRYMAN (FUSILIER)

Sir Robert Wilson, a British military liaison officer who spent years attached to Russian Army HQ, described the typical Russian soldier thus:

The infantry is generally composed of athletic men between the ages of 18 and 40, endowed with great bodily strength, but generally of short stature, with martial countenance and complexion; inured to the extreme of weather and hardship; to the worst and scantiest food; to marches for days and nights, or four hours repose and six hours progress; accustomed to laborious toils, and the carriage of heavy burthens [sic]; ferocious, but disciplined; obstinately brave, and susceptible of enthusiastic excitements; devoted to their sovereign, their chief, and their country. Religious without being weakened by superstition; patient, docile, and obedient; possessing all the energetic characteristics of a barbarian people, with the advantages engrafted by civilization.

Brett-James, *1812*, p. 73

Russian soldier often fought with a determination bordering on fanaticism; yet his qualities of docility and blinkered outlook deprived him of the capacity for independent thinking or initiative. Moreover, shortages of (infamously poor quality) gunpowder for live-firing exercises rendered him a poor shot and denied new conscripts of at least a rudimentary understanding of conditions in battle. His 1798 pattern musket was much heavier than its French counterpart and, thus significantly more encumbered than both his allies and enemies, may have contributed to the Russian soldier's heavy reliance on the bayonet – a practice underscored by Marshal Suvorov's advocacy of close-quarter fighting in the campaigns against the Poles and Turks in the 1780s and against the French in 1799.

Officers in line regiments tended to hail from the landed gentry, but possessed little education and suffered from poor prospects of promotion, with the higher ranks – characteristic of their counterparts in most other contemporary armies – monopolised by their social betters. Although they received some training as cadets, officers tended towards indifference to their professional responsibilities, with many opting for posts at headquarters to avoid the more demanding requirements of regimental duties. According to Sir Robert Wilson, a British liaison officer attached to the Russian Army over the course of several campaigns:

> The Russian officer, although frequently making the greatest physical exertions, is, however, inclined to indolent habits when not on actual duty; loves his sleep after food, and dislikes to walk or ride far.

> Brett-James, *1812*, p. 73

Many officers enlisted as children, taking up their commissions – sometimes well above that of ensign or cornet, the equivalent of second lieutenant in the infantry or cavalry, respectively – during their teens, and thus sometimes commanding a company or squadron with no field experience whatsoever.

Infantry regiments consisted of musketeers, grenadiers or *jäger*. Musketeers functioned as ordinary line infantry, with grenadiers, as in other armies, at least in theory composed of elite troops – generally physically more imposing and trained specifically to carry out assaults, though without, as their name implied, employing grenades, which had fallen into disuse decades earlier. *Jäger* consisted of light infantrymen who could operate in open or formed order as the need arose – the equivalent of Austrian *grenzers* or French *voltigeurs*. In all, the infantry was organised into thirteen grenadier regiments and seventy-seven musketeer regiments, each of three battalions, with each in turn containing four companies of 154 men each (616 in total). The *jäger* regiments numbered twenty, also of three battalions each, but with smaller companies, each containing 104 men.

Russian cavalry was noted for its fine-quality mounts and the large size of their regiments, with dragoons and cuirassiers

INACCURACY OF FIREARMS

All infantry at Austerlitz carried a smoothbore musket or *fusil*
with a rate of fire of about two rounds a minute, but all such
weapons suffered from poor accuracy. One British officer
of the period noted that a soldier armed with a standard
musket, which varied little between armies:

… will strike a figure of a man at 80 yards – it may even
… at 100, but a soldier must be very unfortunate indeed
who shall be wounded by a common musket at 150 yards
provided his antagonist aims at him: and as to firing at a man
at 200 yards with a common musket, you may as well fire at
the moon and have the same hope of hitting your object.
I do maintain and will prove whenever called upon that
no man was ever killed at 200 yards by a common
musket by the person who aimed at him.

Hughes, *Firepower*, p. 26

boasting an official strength of a thousand men, and hussar and
uhlan regiments numbering as high as 1,800, though shortages
of horses reduced these significantly in practice. The army in 1805
included six regiments of cuirassiers, twenty-six of dragoons, nine of
hussars and four of *uhlans*. Heavy cavalry regiments contained five
squadrons plus half a squadron at the regimental depot for purposes
of recruitment and the furnishing of new drafts to the regiment in
the field. Light cavalry regiments consisted of ten squadrons plus
one depot squadron. The Russians also deployed the infamous
Cossacks, irregular horsemen from the steppes of the Ukraine, the
Don River basin, the Crimea and elsewhere. While of very limited use
in a stand-up fight, these colourful if undisciplined men excelled at
scouting, harassment and raiding – not to mention looting.

The artillery was numerous and well manned, with crews
generally prepared to die at their guns rather than withdraw in
the face of attack. The Russians operated a disproportionately
large number of heavy calibre pieces, in particular 12-pounders,
so called because of the weight of the shot they fired.

Like the French, the Russians maintained their own Imperial Guard – an elite, all-arms formation whose infantry component consisted of three regiments of grenadiers, one of four battalions and the others of three, and one battalion of *jäger*. The Guard cavalry contained two heavy regiments – the Life Guard Horse and the Chevalier Guard – one regiment of hussars and two squadrons of Cossacks. All told, the Imperial Guard numbered eleven battalions, seventeen squadrons and forty guns. In populating their officer corps, the Imperial Guard drew heavily on the aristocracy and young men of otherwise high birth with connections at court, irrespective of their level of competence in the field. In this respect they shared little in common with their French counterparts, the latter of whom earned their place through a meritocratic system and years of field experience.

Though numerous and basically of good stock, the Russian Army nevertheless suffered from inadequate transport, a poor system of supply and a dearth of experience in manoeuvring large formations in a co-ordinated fashion. Moreover, the shift of regiments and brigades between divisions resulted in an inability of commanders at all levels to develop close relationships with their men or a capacity to command and exercise their unit as an effectively unchanging, cohesive formation. Still, next to the French, it was the largest army in Europe; however, while the total of all Russian forces across the empire in 1805 amounted to 343 battalions and 297 squadrons, supplemented by garrison units and irregulars, its commitments across the vast area of territory stretching from the borders of Prussia, Austria and Turkey to the wastes of Siberia left only two-thirds of the army available for active service in Germany, Hanover and Naples – in all, 212 battalions and 207 squadrons.

THE DAYS
BEFORE BATTLE

Opposing Plans

The Allies began to draw up a grand strategic plan for the coming campaign in July 1805, although Pitt had already laid out his ideas as early as January. The plan envisioned several simultaneous offensives involving a total of about 500,000 men operating on different fronts across the Continent. In the north, a British expeditionary force of 15,000 men would land in Hanover, supported by 12,000 Swedes and 20,000 Russians concentrating in Stralsund, the main town in Swedish Pomerania, on the north German coast. Linking up with these, in due course, General Bennigsen would bring 50,000 Russian troops from the Vistula River, in Russian Poland, with further forces to assemble in Riga under Generals Buxhöwden and Michelson. These forces would serve a double purpose: reinforcing Allied efforts further west, but also encouraging Prussia to throw in her lot with the coalition by furnishing the 200,000 troops at her disposal. The tsar would request free passage of his troops across Prussian soil but, if refused, Russian forces planned to march west through Hungary and Austria en route to the western Danube in Bavaria.

Indeed, as the Allies regarded Bavaria as one of the main theatres of operation, the Austrian General Mack and Archduke

THE DEBATE OVER WAR PREPAREDNESS

Owing to the Austrian Army's poor state of readiness for war, Archduke Charles strongly advised against hostilities in 1805, arguing that six months' preparation was required to put the army on a war footing, since the reforms initiated in the wake of the disastrous campaign of 1800 had yet to bear fruit. He also cited the unreliability of the Russians, who had unilaterally abandoned the Second Coalition in 1799. Nor did he place much stock in the diversionary potential promised by British expeditionary operations on the Continent, since he reckoned that Italy or Germany must inevitably constitute the main focus of the Allied effort. Convinced that the army could be made ready in as little as two months, and exercising their considerable influence at court, the joint foreign ministers, Franz Colloredo and Johann Cobenzl, together with General Mack, overrode Charles – the emperor's brother, no less – with fatal results to the Austrian cause.

Ferdinand, with 85,000 troops, would occupy this south German state, while 85,000 Russians under General Kutuzov would follow up, rendezvous with their Austrian allies and proceed toward the Rhine from Ulm. In northern Italy, meanwhile, Archduke John with 25,000 Austrians would occupy the Tyrol and the passes through the Alps, with the expectation of moving north into Bavaria or further south in Italy as events required. As the Allies expected northern Italy to become the focus of the main French thrust – historically consistent with the campaigns of 1796–97 and 1800 – Archduke Charles, with 100,000 troops, would operate in that region, defeat the Franco-Italian forces under Eugène de Beauharnais, retake Lombardy and proceed into south-western France. In the Mediterranean, a combined Anglo-Russian force of 17,000 men was to land in Naples, there to join 36,000 Neapolitan troops arriving by sea from Sicily in order to liberate King Ferdinand IV's mainland Italian possession. This achieved, the Allies would march north to co-ordinate their efforts with Archduke

Austerlitz 1805

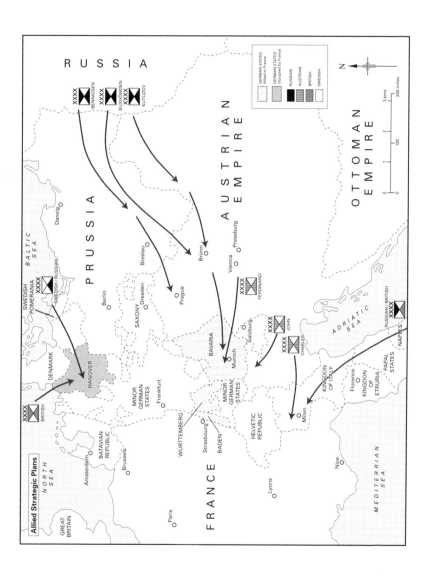

Charles. If circumstances looked favourable, Britain would launch diversionary operations in western France and Holland, and would provide aid to revolts they hoped to stimulate in Brittany and the Vendée in support of the exiled Bourbon dynasty.

Thus, the Allies formulated a plan on a vast scale, with operations to be undertaken across Europe intended to divert the French in the north, south and west, while the Allied main effort concentrated in southern Germany and northern Italy.

The French were not ignorant of Allied intentions and therefore laid their own plans accordingly, with an eye to striking a rapid, decisive blow by seizing the initiative early in the campaign. Napoleon could field approximately 250,000 experienced troops, plus another 150,000 recruits. Most of the former stood along the Channel coast, while others occupied garrisons far afield: Hanover, Holland, Piedmont and Naples, as well as in France. With such dispersion of troops, fewer than 100,000 men were on hand to protect the nation's borders and those of its allies; yet in order to confront forces numbering several times his own, Napoleon appreciated that he must cancel his planned invasion of Britain, break up most of the camps around Boulogne and dispatch the new Grande Armée south-east, ultimately to strike pre-emptively in order to compensate for his numerical inferiority. Speed and surprise were to figure heavily in his plans, for he needed to execute a decisive blow before the Allies could bring the bulk of their troops to bear.

Napoleon believed the Allies' vulnerable point lay along the western Danube where, as discussed, Austrian forces intended to operate with a view to occupying Bavaria – so blocking French access through the Black Forest and other routes into Moravia, the region around Vienna. Bavaria served as a natural target for the French offensive, since Napoleon could cast himself as the defender of a minor state. Operations would involve over 200,000 troops moving in a massive concentric arc consisting of seven corps advancing from various directions in co-ordinated fashion. By maintaining mutually supporting distances between each corps, Napoleon recognised the feasibility of his forces converging on the Danube in the region of Münster, Donauwörth and Ingolstadt, so placing overwhelming numbers in a position to encircle Mack's army before Kutuzov could link up with it. On other fronts, Marshal Brune, with 30,000 troops, would remain along the Channel to protect it from a British amphibious raid, Gouvion St Cyr would defend Naples and, finally, Masséna, with 50,000 men, would monitor Archduke Charles in northern Italy, keeping him from influencing operations along the Danube.

Denouement in Bavaria: The Ulm Campaign

The Allies made several false assumptions from the outset. First, they failed to anticipate Napoleon's ability or intention to abandon the invasion of Britain in the event of Austrian mobilisation. Second, and worse still, General Mack's strong recommendation that the army not mobilise until absolutely ready so as to avoid provoking a French military response failed to account for the fact that the troops in and around Boulogne already stood on a war footing, and thus could be on the move the moment they received orders from the emperor accordingly. The Austrians also wrongly presumed that the Elector of Bavaria would support the Allies, being ignorant of on-going negotiations between Paris and Munich concerning a Franco-Bavarian alliance.

On 6 August, Mack learned that the Russians under Kutuzov would arrive later than expected and in weaker numbers. This did not deter Mack from proceeding on the basis of existing plans, overriding Archduke Charles' view that the Austrians make no moves until the Russians linked up with them. According to Mack's calculations, the French could not engage Austrian forces in Bavaria in fewer than sixty-eight days, whereas he estimated the arrival of Kutuzov at Braunau to occur in under sixty-five. These calculations proved faulty, reflecting an inaccurate understanding of the speed of movement of troops over poor roads and a failure to appreciate the French Army's superior speed of march over all its rivals. Not only, therefore, did Mack persuade Emperor Francis of these figures' accuracy, but when the former issued orders for his army to proceed towards Bavaria, unbeknownst to him Napoleon's troops had left their camps along the coast more than a week earlier.

Austrian movements from their camp at Wels began on 5 September and three days later the advance guard of the Army of Germany crossed the River Inn en route for the vicinity of Ulm, where it intended to establish a fortified camp, thereby controlling the direct route between France and Austria. Mack encountered no resistance from the Bavarians, who withdrew to the north-west, but this was as expected, as Bavaria had traditionally allowed the Austrians unhindered right of passage in their various wars against France in the past – most recently during the campaign of 1799 – not least owing to the fact that Francis held the title of Holy Roman Emperor, as well as Emperor of Austria. When, therefore, the elector altered his country's traditional policy and actually sided with the French, this caught the Austrians completely unprepared, enabling Napoleon to use the Austrian 'invasion' of Bavaria as a pretext for moving against Mack before the other Allied armies were ready to implement their campaign plans. Increasing the Allies' discomfiture, Mack's plan to speed his advance by mimicking the French tradition of 'living off the land' proved a dismal failure, for the Austrians possessed no experience of foraging on this scale, as a consequence of which many men found themselves deprived of sufficient food, the advance made poor progress and discipline suffered.

As Mack's forces proceeded through Bavaria, the Russians marched through Austrian Galicia (now part of Poland), though at a considerably slower pace owing to the radical difference in road quality between those in Western versus Eastern Europe and the dearth of parallel thoroughfares. The Russian advance consequently became extended along the same stretch of road shared by all formations, rendering their rate of march considerably slower than that of the French, who did not labour under these

Austerlitz 1805

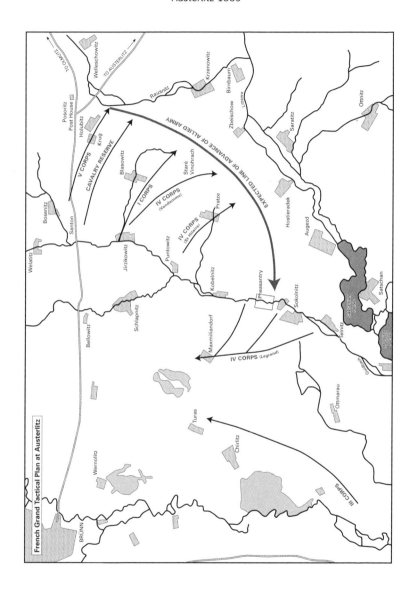

French Grand Tactical Plan at Austerlitz

conditions far to the west. As a result, whereas by the end of September Mack's forces had reached the area around Ulm, the Russian advance guard was still only at Teschen, with elements of Kutuzov's army diverted through Moldavia as a consequence of a possible hostile move by the Turks. Moreover, notwithstanding large numbers of carts provided by the Austrians at Teschen, even the increased pace through Moravia and into the Danube Valley still rendered an impossibility the arrival of Kutuzov's army in Bavaria on the heels of their allies.

The Grande Armée broke camp at Boulogne on 27 August, its advanced guard reaching the Rhine on 25 September. Napoleon planned to move his troops from the Channel coast to Bavaria with all possible speed, with the intention of striking at Mack's Austrians through a turning movement against his right flank and a descent upon his rear, thereby both denying him reinforcements from Austria and, above all, reaching and destroying his forces before the arrival of the Russians. Napoleon deployed five corps along the Rhine, stretching from Mayence (Mainz) to Strasbourg, plus another under Marshal Bernadotte – drawn mostly from forces occupying Hanover – on the east side of the Rhine near Hesse-Kassel. The French began crossing the Rhine on the same day they arrived there, on 25 September, deploying a cavalry screen in the Black Forest as a ruse to deceive the Austrians into believing that the French were moving west. In all, six corps advanced along parallel routes with orders to converge on the Danube between Ulm and Ingolstadt.

As rival forces advanced against one another, Napoleon was active on the diplomatic front, concluding alliances with Württemberg and Baden, which agreed to furnish troops for the campaign, and cementing Franco-Bavarian co-operation with the promise of two further divisions. The French conducted their advance with remarkable speed despite shortages of horses for the transport of all the artillery and ammunition wagons, covering over 125 miles (200km) in approximately twelve days. The main body reached the Danube on 7 October, with the various corps positioned along the Danube to Günzburg and Bernadotte's I Corps, together with the Bavarian contingent, occupying positions near Ingolstadt.

The direction of march conducted by I Corps was to have unforeseen diplomatic repercussions, for in seeking to increase his pace, Bernadotte marched through the Prussian enclave of Ansbach instead of taking the more circuitous route around it, thereby violating neutral territory. This excited hawks in Berlin, but in making vociferous objections they inadvertently placed Frederick William in an awkward position, for by failing neither to oppose Bernadotte's advance nor to declare war on France, Prussia faced charges of duplicity, having already refused Tsar Alexander's troops access through Prussian territory in the east in order to speed their advance to the front.

On 9 October French troops crossed the Danube as soon as they reached it, though the first encounter with the Austrians occurred the day before at Wertingen, where cavalry under Murat inflicted heavy casualties on a detachment, prisoners from which revealed that Mack remained to the west. Ney's VI Corps met resistance at Günzburg, but the other corps crossed the river for the most part without resistance. I Corps and the Bavarians proceeded east for the purpose of blocking any reinforcements from reaching the Allied main body, while the other formations executed manoeuvres which prevented escape from Ulm. IV Corps under Soult reached Memmingen, south of Ulm, on the 13th; II Corps under Marmont manoeuvred on Soult's right; Lannes' V and Ney's VI Corps, together with the Cavalry Reserve under Murat, proceeded west for Ulm.

Advised to try to break out of the trap which was rapidly closing in on him, Mack sent a probing force of approximately 23,000 men down the north bank of the Danube to scout out a line of retreat, encountering General Dupont's division from VI Corps, between Haslach and Jungingen. Outnumbered, yet fighting with considerable energy, Dupont's men were forced to retreat after inflicting heavy casualties on the Austrians, who withdrew to Ulm.

The westward movement of the French now convinced Mack that they were bound for France to quell a reported coup and to repel a British landing. Both these stories proved false, and while Mack sat idle for two days, the French concentrated their forces in preparation for an envelopment.

Mack did not act until 14 October, with a blaze of orders which sought to extricate his army by breaking out to the north. Accordingly, General Riesch moved along the north bank of the Danube, only to be intercepted by Ney at Elchingen, where the French forced him back to Ulm. A second corps, under Werneck, marched north, followed by Murat's cavalry. Mack, sensing imminent catastrophe, became incapable of making a decision, so that on the night of 14/15 October, 6,000 cavalry left Ulm under Prince Schwarzenberg and Archduke Ferdinand with the intention of linking up with Werneck – and thus leaving Mack to cope as best he could in Ulm. There the French completed their encirclement on the 15th, with Ney west of the city, where he

Capitulation at Jungingen, 11 October. One of a number of instances prior to Austerlitz when sizeable Austrian formations surrendered to pursuing French forces. Exerting continuous pressure on their opponents constituted a hallmark of French strategy in the 1805 campaign.

stormed the outer redoubts and established himself in a position to bombard Mack's doomed army.

In this strong position, on the 17th, Napoleon's aide de camp, the comte de Ségur, went to Mack to negotiate the Austrian surrender. Mack agreed on condition that reinforcements did not arrive by 25 October, since Mack expected the Russians imminently, providing 35,000 men under Kutuzov's command, possibly to be joined by 18,000 further east, plus Werneck's corps of 9,000. But if he thought that his force, even in combination with these others, could possibly confront and force back almost 200,000 French and Bavarians, he was quite mistaken, not least with circumstances rapidly deteriorating for the Austrians. In the event, Murat made contact with Werneck's corps on 18 October, forcing it to capitulate at Trochtelfingen. At the same time, within Ulm itself, morale sunk as a consequence of the departure of Ferdinand and Schwarzenberg and the knowledge of Mack's exchanges with the French, which confirmed their fears: on 19 October he capitulated, his forces laying down their arms the following day, with the loss of fifty-one battalions, eighteen squadrons and sixty guns – about 25,000 men, all told. In all, the Austrians lost 50,000 men of the 72,000 who had marched into Bavaria.

In a matter of two months, the Grande Armée had decamped from Boulogne and appeared in Bavaria with such rapidity as to overwhelm an entire Austrian army, throwing into confusion the Allied campaign plan. Napoleon had seized the initiative and dealt a severe, though not yet decisive, blow to the forces of the Third Coalition, depriving it of the (Austrian) Army of Germany and leaving behind only a combination of small detachments and some larger formations, but none which the French could either pursue or at least keep under observation. These included a division under Jellacic operating to the south on detachment from the Army of the Tyrol. After being cut off, it was obliged to retreat back into the mountains, combining with other formations called up from southern Tyrol and Italy. General Kienmayer's 18,000 men operating north of Ulm now had to withdraw behind

The capitulation at Ulm: the culmination of the one of the greatest strategic envelopments in military history. Even more spectacular examples of encirclement on a grand scale would occur at Sedan in 1870 and at Stalingrad in 1943.

the Inn, where they linked up with the newly arrived Russians under Kutuzov, he having arrived at Braunau on 9 October. By the 26th, Kutuzov mustered 27,000 men, with a further 11,000 stragglers stretched along an extended line of march marked by the exhausted and ill. With Mack's army disposed of, it now fell to Napoleon to confront the Russians.

From Ulm to the Eve of Austerlitz

The capitulation at Ulm, together with the surrenders at Haslach-Jungingen (11 October), Memmingen (13 October), Elchingen (14 October) and Trochtelfingen (18 October), signalled the end of Austrian resistance in Bavaria, resulting in the loss of ninety-six battalions and twenty-six squadrons, most of them taken at Ulm. This left the Russians assuming the main, as opposed to

THE BATTLE OF ELCHINGEN, 14 OCTOBER

Although not present at Austerlitz, Marshal Michel Ney played an instrumental part in the campaign by closing the ring around Mack's Austrian Army in Bavaria. Employing only 7,500 men from his corps, he attacked 15,000 Austrians under Graf von Riesch at Elchingen, a small village north-east of Ulm. Undaunted by the superior numbers opposing him, Ney drove back the defenders, crossed the heavily damaged bridge – literally as engineers struggled to repair it – and successfully stormed the village. Ney lost 1,600 killed and 1,400 wounded to the Austrians' 4,000 casualties, of whom 2,500 became prisoners.

the supporting, role in confronting the French, but with help yet to be drawn from Kienmayer's corps and various scattered detachments. In light of the disaster at Ulm, the Austrians began to assemble these various elements, calling in far-flung garrisons from across the empire, replacing them with reserve battalions, accelerating recruitment and bringing in frontier troops from along the border with Turkey. The Russians, too, were obliged to change their plans, reorganising troops along the Prussian frontier, yet still watching to ensure that Frederick William did not take advantage of the absence of Russian forces. It is noteworthy that, in spite of the close relationship between the Russian and Prussian monarchs, resentment by the latter remained as a consequence of Prussia having been denied all the Polish territory she desired during the Second and Third Partitions of Poland in 1793 and 1795, respectively.

Notwithstanding the severe blow dealt to the Third Coalition by the capitulation at Ulm, Napoleon still faced approximately 300,000 Allies on a number of fronts, although the speed of his advance through Bavaria had by now thrown into disarray his opponents' campaign timetable, and without the ability to concentrate the majority of those otherwise impressive numbers

1805: The Naval Dimension

In pursuing Napoleon's plans for the invasion of England, in March Admiral Villeneuve and his fleet broke out of the British naval blockade of Toulon and proceeded to rendezvous with a Spanish squadron at Cádiz before sailing to the West Indies. There the combined Franco-Spanish force hoped to establish contact with the French fleet out of Brest, reinforced by other Spanish vessels. The plan operated on the premise that the British would pursue but fail to locate their quarry, allowing time for Villeneuve to return to European waters undetected – and thus free to clear the Channel in June or July, so enabling the invasion force at Boulogne to cross unopposed. The plan did not succeed. Vice Admiral Horatio Nelson did pursue Villeneuve – and did lose touch near Martinique – but the Brest fleet had failed to break the British blockade, and thus Villeneuve returned to European waters with a smaller force than expected. He consequently sailed for Ferrol, on the north-western coast of Spain, hoping to link up with a Spanish squadron there before sailing north in hopes of breaking the blockade of Brest, adding that fleet to his own before continuing on to the Channel. However, by a chance encounter between Admiral Calder's squadron and Villeneuve's off the Spanish coast, the latter was obliged to put in to port at Vigo. Nelson, meanwhile, gave up his search in the West Indies and sailed for Gibraltar before returning to Portsmouth. As such, the Franco-Spanish lost their opportunity to clear the Channel and the planned invasion of Britain came to naught. Although thwarted in this respect, these changed circumstances enabled Napoleon to re-direct the troops camped along the Channel coast for operations in Germany against the forces of the Third Coalition.

THE BATTLE OF AMSTETTEN, 5 NOVEMBER

Following Mack's surrender at Ulm, Kutuzov ordered a rapid retreat on 4 November, leaving Bagration with about 8,000 troops as a rear guard to delay the French. General Nicolas Oudinot's converged grenadier division, advancing through thick snow, drove back two lines of defence, but reinforcements under Miloradovich entered the fray, stubbornly holding his position before eventually withdrawing through the village of Amstetten. He lost 2,000 casualties but, crucially, had enabled Kutuzov's main body to continue its movement east.

in a single theatre of operation, the Allied offensive appeared far more imposing on paper than in the field. The British, at least, could take a small degree of solace when, the day following Mack's surrender, Vice Admiral Horatio Nelson decisively defeated the combined Franco-Spanish fleet under Villeneuve at Trafalgar, off the Spanish coast, thereby safeguarding Britain's shores for the foreseeable future; but this was not known for more than two weeks and in any event made no impression on events in Central Europe.

Napoleon's first priority in the wake of Ulm was to pursue the Russians under Kutuzov, who, upon learning of Mack's debacle, immediately ordered his troops to retreat over the River Inn. Having regrouped his forces around Munich and Landshut, on the 26th the emperor began his pursuit. With 36,000 Russians and 22,000 Austrians, Kutuzov desperately sought to cross to the north bank of the Danube and rendezvous with the 30,000 reinforcements approaching from the east under Buxhöwden. Despite their reputation for remarkable speed, the French failed to catch the withdrawing Russians, apart from a few rear-guard actions fought at various river lines after they passed the Inn on the 28th. At the Enns, Napoleon created a provisional corps of

The Battle of Dürnstein, 11 November 1805. One of several engagements fought between Kutuzov's rear guard and pursuing French troops.

KUTUZOV'S RETREAT

News of the disaster at Ulm reached Kutuzov on 23 October when Mack, on parole, rode into Russian headquarters and reported it. Although recently reinforced with Austrian troops, which increased his force to 50,000 men, Kutuzov abandoned plans for an advance into Bavaria and on the 26th began moving east back down the Danube Valley toward Vienna, leaving Kienmayer to destroy the bridge over the River Inn to slow up the French. The route Kutuzov employed provided him with a series of defensible positions, including several rivers which a rear guard could hold to delay the French pursuit, as they would at Hollabrunn, Amstettin, Dürnstein and elsewhere.

divisions detached from three corps, assigning command to Marshal Mortier, who was to advance along the northern bank of the Danube, although the wide dispersal of these divisions left Mortier with only one for some time. On other fronts, Ney fought off an attack by Archduke John near Innsbruck, and in northern Italy, Masséna fought indecisively at Caldiero near Verona on

29–30 October, resulting in the Austrians withdrawing behind the River Tagliamento to assist in Archduke John's withdrawal from the Tyrol.

Kutuzov continued to keep a distance between himself and the pursuing French, such that by 9 November he had crossed the Danube near Krems and united with reinforcements numbering 10,000 men. Thus augmented, he struck Mortier at Dürnstein on the 11th with 15,000 men, but late in the day reinforcements enabled Mortier to hold back his attackers. Napoleon bitterly regretted that Mortier received no substantial assistance from his fellow marshals, particularly Murat, but on the other hand, the latter commander managed to bluff the Austrians to forfeit intact a bridge over the Danube in Vienna by falsely claiming that his superiors had concluded an armistice. While the Austrians listened to Murat spin his yarn, with Lannes at his side to corroborate the story, French grenadiers rushed the bridge, disarming the defenders without bloodshed. At the same time, discovering that Kutuzov was withdrawing north in the direction of Znaim, Napoleon ordered Bernadotte to cross the Danube at Molk; Murat's cavalry and V and VI Corps to traverse the river via the Tabor bridge; and Davout to follow up from the rear and occupy Vienna. Reaching the capital on the 15th, Napoleon continued to hope he could engage Kutuzov before he united with Buxhöwden.

It was not to be, for the Russians, in their turn, managed to fool the French when, at Hollabrünn on 15 November, General Bagration, the commander of the rear guard, tricked Murat into believing an armistice had been arranged. By the time Napoleon disabused Murat of this falsehood, Murat could only attack belatedly, unable to prevent Bagration, despite some loss inflicted upon him in the course of the day, from withdrawing intact across the bridge at Schöngraben – and thus failing to prevent the Russian joining his compatriots. More worryingly for the French, on 20 November Kutuzov finally joined forces with Buxhöwden, raising the strength of the main Russian Army to 86,000 troops. On the other hand, elsewhere the Austrians'

Murat and Lannes surprising the Austrians at the Tabor bridge on the outskirts of Vienna, 14 November.

Viennese officials granting Napoleon the keys to the city. The fall of the Habsburg capital did not mark a decisive shift in the campaign, but demonstrated rather further evidence of Austria's inability after Ulm to stem the French advance towards Moravia.

conduct did not promise to compensate much for the loss of Mack's army, for an intercepted dispatch indicated that Archduke Charles' force, lightly shadowed by Masséna, would probably not reach Leoben, the position occupied by II Corps under Marmont, before the 24th. Other significant Austrian formations were also under pressure from French commanders determined to prevent them from intervening in the main theatre of operations in Moravia. Specifically, in the Tyrol, Ney and the Bavarian contingent continued to pursue Archduke John, who had little choice but to retreat in the face of superior numbers. Thus confident that his southern flank stood secure, Napoleon could concentrate on his advance north against the Russians.

Napoleon reached Znaim on the 17th, now persuaded that he could not engage Kutuzov before he linked up with other Russian formations. Fatigue plagued the emperor's troops, moreover, and he knew he must cease the pursuit and allow his various corps to rest and reorganise. His predicament did not end there, for although he was unaware of the precise terms of the Treaty of Potsdam (3 November), by which Prussia agreed to join the Allies on 15 December if Napoleon refused their peace terms, he was aware of Prussian mobilisation, which with little notice could present him with a new adversary boasting up to 200,000 troops. Napoleon, on the other hand, possessed no more than 53,000 immediately available men, for prudence dictated the detachment of various formations to guard his lines of communication and to garrison key points, most notably Vienna. With the Grande Armée now 700 miles (1,126km) from home soil and nearing the end of its operational lifeline, on 23 November the emperor ordered it to halt at Brünn, about 35 miles (56km) north of Vienna. Bernadotte's I Corps, plus the Bavarians under Wrede, were to assemble in and around Iglau, north-west of Brünn, there to watch for any Prussian moves from the north and to observe the 18,000 men under Archduke Ferdinand, who it will be recalled escaped Mack's fate and was reckoned to be en route from Prague to Brünn.

Napoleon, facing an officer of elite carabiniers, studies the ground at Brünn, west of Austerlitz. In this, as in many previous and subsequent campaigns, the emperor took great pains to choose ground which he could employ to his advantage on the day of battle.

The French emperor's predicament also included the possibility that Archdukes Charles and John could conceivably advance from the south at a time when Napoleon – his own formations not yet concentrated and temperatures plummeting – remained too short of troops with which to engage the combined Allied army concentrating around Olmütz, approximately 45 miles (72km) north-east of Brünn. The personal presence of Tsar Alexander and Emperor Francis, moreover, was certain to have raised Russian and Austrian morale.

With both armies now in close proximity to one another, Napoleon had to ensure that the Russians remained and fought – a prospect that looked favourable since, with the presence of the Austrians, the strategic advantage appeared now to lie with the Allies. His army now deep in the heart of Europe, it was critical that Napoleon achieve a decisive victory, for with the Prussians neutral yet preparing to join the Third Coalition, the Allies stood to crush him through overwhelming numbers alone. Napoleon

Having finalised his plan of attack with his headquarters staff, Napoleon beds down in front of a fire on the evening before Austerlitz.

therefore faced four prospects: first, if Kutuzov chose to beat a hasty retreat and successfully elude the French, Napoleon would be denied the decisive battle he sought, and face no choice but to withdraw, with the Allies left intact. Nor, secondly, would a drawn battle achieve his ends, for again the Allies would remain a continuing, albeit weakened, threat. Thirdly, if Napoleon was obliged to confront a numerically superior enemy force on ground of its own choosing, he would suffer from a serious tactical disadvantage. This left a fourth – and the most viable – option: somehow to persuade the Allies to attack him at a time and place that suited him. This therefore constituted the strategy Napoleon pursued.

Such a course naturally depended on the Russians accepting the bait Napoleon intended to offer, which was to persuade them that they outnumbered him by a factor of two to one and that, suddenly made aware of his predicament, he stood at a loss to respond. As such, Napoleon spent the next ten days pursuing a campaign of bluff and espionage. General Savary was sent to Tsar Alexander's headquarters at Olmütz to assess the Russians' mood and sound them out on the question of a negotiated peace, which he disingenuously suggested the emperor, concerned about his isolated position, was keen to conclude. Moreover, while the Grande Armée sat idle, suggesting indecisiveness, Napoleon sent out aides to bring in the corps of Marshals Davout and Bernadotte and all other formations for the coming battle. At the same time, the emperor, reviewing the campaigns conducted in the area by Frederick the Great in the mid-eighteenth century and examining the maps copiously supplied by his cartographical department, personally rode over the countryside between Brünn and Olmütz, seeking favourable ground on which to confront the Austro-Russian Army. After careful thought he chose a position between Brünn and the small village of Austerlitz, about 13 miles (21km) to the east.

The Allies decided on an offensive battle for the following day, 2 December, employing a plan to fix Napoleon in front of the commanding Pratzen Heights, so leaving him with the impression that he faced the threat of a frontal attack there by numerically superior opponents. In reality, 55,000 men of a total force of 89,000 would move southwards to strike the French right flank between the villages of Telnitz and Sokolnitz. Having crossed the Goldbach stream and penetrated French defences, Buxhöwden's spearhead would extend outwards to cut the French lines of communication with Vienna and encircle Napoleon's army from the rear. In the meantime, the remainder of the Russian forces would hold the line on the right under Bagration, while the Russian Imperial Guard – a mere 10,000 men, but an elite formation – would occupy the Pratzen Heights in the centre under Grand Duke Constantine, the tsar's brother.

As Napoleon intended, the battlefield extended over a small area stretching 16 miles (26km) from Brünn to Austerlitz, but in the event the actual length of the front measured, from north to south, less than 10 miles (16km). The Goldbach and its tributary, the Bosenitz, which crossed the field, constituted nothing more formidable than marsh streams. There were no features of striking elevation save for the Pratzen Heights, but even these rose only 320ft (98m) above sea level. On the northern extreme of the field stood wooded hills, rendering an outflanking movement here impossible to both sides. Between the heights and the main road extending east–west between Brünn and Olmütz stood a 600ft (200m) mound occupied by the French known as the Santon. The Pratzen Heights stood south of the main road, in Russian possession, and provided a commanding view of the battlefield. To the south lay the villages of Kobelnitz, Sokolnitz and Telnitz; the Goldbach meandered through boggy water meadows in which lay a number of small shallow lakes, most prominently the Satchan pond – all frozen over.

Napoleon's basic plan was to encourage the Allies to outflank him to the south, where he had deliberately weakened his right wing. By doing so, they would be risking exposing their own flank on the Pratzen Heights as they executed this manoeuvre. To encourage the Allies to assume this risk, the emperor would

Napoleon and one of his aides de camp examining a map on the eve of Austerlitz.

abandon the heights, feigning nervousness. Key to his stratagem was the Santon, which was to be preserved in French hands at all costs, and whose fortification by the French prior to the battle strongly suggested to his opponents that Napoleon intended to remain static and await an Allied frontal attack at the northern end of his line. By weakening his defences between Kobelnitz and Telnitz, Napoleon deliberately sought to entice an Allied attack there. But the emperor had no intention of remaining on the defensive, for he would form up behind the centre of the line 30,000 men under Soult, supported by Bernadotte's corps and the vaunted Imperial Guard. None of these formations would be observable to their opponents.

As soon as the Allies had begun their flanking march and removed most of their troops from the Pratzen Heights, Soult would assault them, seizing a position previously deemed virtually unassailable and therefore the point at which an attack would least be expected. If he succeeded, Napoleon would then encircle his

French Army bivouac on the night of 1 December.

THE ROLE OF INTELLIGENCE

Charles Schulmeister, a Strasbourg trader, spied very effectively for the French, adopting a disguise and accompanying General Savary clandestinely to examine the roads running from the Rhine, north of the Black Forest, to the Danube. Through various contacts, above all an aide-de-camp to the Austrian general Kienmayer, Schulmeister supplied largely worthless information on French movements to Allied commanders, but acquired in return valuable intelligence on the state of Austrian and Russian troops. Armed with a pass from the Austrians, Schulmeister acquired an Austrian officer's uniform and moved freely amidst Allied lines, learning much about their intentions and strength, and dispatching a lengthy report to Napoleon in late October. After being betrayed on the 30th by an Austrian customs officer whom he tried to recruit, Schulmeister was arrested and left for dead after being beaten by his guards during transit between prisons. He recovered and returned to French lines, carrying out still further intelligence work in the course of the campaign.

enemy from the rear, pushing back Allied formations against the Menitz and Satchan ponds. Having destroyed the Austro-Russian main body, he would then shift northwards to attack Bagration's force, which Marshals Murat and Lannes would have engaged on the left (northern sector) of the French line. By nightfall on 1 December, the emperor had shifted his troops in accordance with the movements of the Austro-Russians southwards, as he desired. Both sides now stood poised for battle, confident of success on the morrow.

THE BATTLEFIELD:
WHAT ACTUALLY HAPPENED?

Allied Attacks on Telnitz and Sokolnitz

2 December 1805		
	0700hrs	Sunrise. Kienmayer commences his attack on the village of Telnitz
	0830hrs	Allies capture Telnitz
	0900hrs	Langeron begins attack against Sokolnitz
	0930hrs	Russians assault the castle and pheasantry
	0945hrs	The French are ejected from Sokolnitz, though sporadic skirmish fire continues in the pheasantry and west of the village

Action commenced at 0700hrs with the Allied attack on Telnitz, a village and its environs on the southern sector held by the French 3rd Line and Piedmontese light troops, the *Tirailleurs du Po*, with a combined strength of about 2,000 men, plus 650 cavalry, who fought for as long as possible so that Napoleon could work on the plan for the main attack to the north. By delaying the Allies and occupying as many of their forces as possible, the French were more likely to succeed in the grand manner Napoleon envisioned for the battle. The French held a line up to the crest of the hill to the village's front, as well as the village itself, with two regiments of cavalry deployed to the south to watch for a flank attack the Allies might launch.

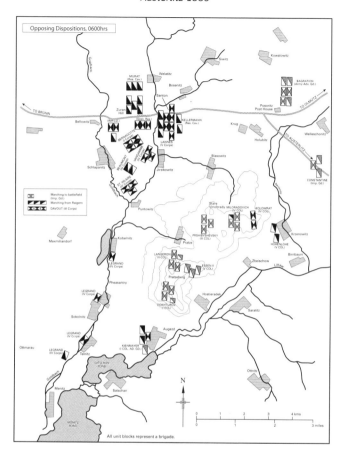

Opposing Dispositions, 0600hrs

All unit blocks represent a brigade.

The Allies meanwhile began to implement the plan formulated, described earlier, by the Austrian general, Weyrother. General Kienmayer, for whom Telnitz represented a prime objective, was meant to use his advance guard in a wide manoeuvre to sweep around the flank and rear of the French, so severing Napoleon's communications with the Austrian capital. However, as a preliminary stage, he needed to capture Telnitz, to the west of which stood the plain of Turas, in which the remainder of the Allied left would operate, allowing the 1st Column to execute the planned sweeping movement. At 0630hrs Kienmayer's men stood assembled at Augezd, 3 miles (5km) east of Telnitz, ready to advance at dawn, with little opposition expected from the French in Telnitz, which formed one of several defensive posts stretching north–south that Napoleon hoped to use in his plan to pin the southern part of the Allied army while swinging round its right. The village stood on the left (or eastern) bank of the Goldbach stream – not an impressive obstacle to infantry, but deep enough to require the use of bridges by cavalry and artillery. Immediately to the east of the village stood a hill which hid the place from view when approaching from the east, and with the French occupying vineyards and orchards as well as houses with walled gardens, a church and a ditch at the bottom of the hill, this deployment added to the strength of the place from an eastern approach. The defenders enjoyed good defensive positions, but conversely a poor one for cavalry. South of the village, about 650 yards (600m) away, stood the frozen Satchan pond. Two bridges stretched across the Goldbach at Telnitz. In all, the village offered an excellent defensive position which enabled a small force, particularly if screened by skirmishers, to delay a larger attacker, and the narrow confines of the space between the Goldbach and the Satchan pond provided only a narrow frontage for an attacker. This was extended further south by the fact that the Satchan pond, as well as the Monitz pond beyond it, blocked easy advance for more than 2.5 miles (4km). Although they were frozen and theoretically traversable, the thickness of the ice was unlikely to be able to bear the weight of cavalry or artillery, much less large formations of infantry.

The sun rose at about 0700hrs, though most of the French position remained covered in mist and fog, concealing the defenders' numbers and rendering their position at Telnitz all the more difficult to assess from Allied lines. Indeed, Kienmayer underestimated the strength of French numbers in the area. Fighting began when a *grenzer* battalion began to engage the skirmishers in the vineyards, the French bringing up reinforcements from the village and inflicting enough casualties on the Austrians

Austerlitz 1805

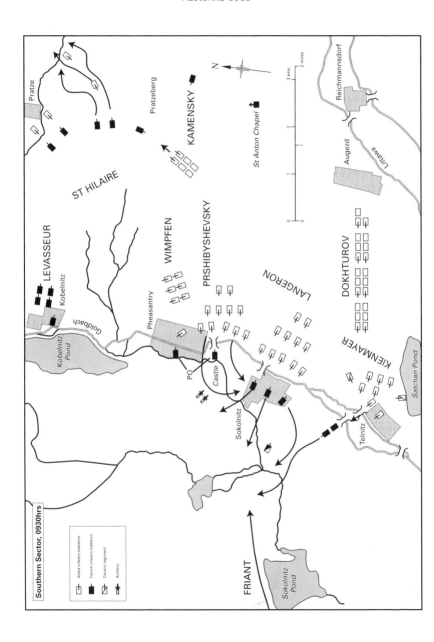

Southern Sector, 0930hrs

Legend:
- Allied infantry battalion
- French infantry battalion
- Cavalry regiment
- Artillery

Labels: Pratze, Pratzeberg, KAMENSKY, ST HILAIRE, LEVASSEUR, Kobelnitz, Goldbach, Kobelnitz Pond, WIMPFEN, Pheasantry, PRSHIBYSHEVSKY, LANGERON, DOKHTUROV, KIENMAYER, Satchan Pond, PO, Castle, Sokolnitz, Telnitz, Sokolnitz Pond, FRIANT, St Anton Chapel, Augezd, Reichmannsdorf, Littawa to oblige their withdrawal. Sending another battalion in support of the first, with three more in reserve, as well as cavalry (totalling about 2,300 infantry and 2,200 cavalry), Kienmayer pushed forward to observe their French counterparts, no more than 2,000 men, on the opposite side of the Goldbach. French infantry occupying the ditch in front of the village repulsed the second

Marshal Louis Davout, commander of III Corps. His defensive posture around the village of Sokolnitz, combined with his timely counter-attacks, contributed strongly to preventing the Allies from crossing the Goldbach and thrusting north, as they had intended.

Austrian attack, while the Austrian cavalry could do nothing in support against infantry protected by the cover of walls and vines. A third attack came forward, finally obliging the French to withdraw from the ditch and vineyards, and into the village itself, where they made use of houses and walled gardens to establish a new line of defence. By this time Kienmayer had already taken substantial losses, with one of the two battalions suffering 50 per cent casualties – a remarkable testimony to the strength of French resistance and the accuracy of their musketry. Undaunted, Kienmayer ordered forward a further three battalions in hopes of seizing the village; accordingly, at 0800hrs, two battalions of *grenzers* rushed furiously towards their objective.

The attackers took heavy fire from the French, only to reel back from their losses, whereupon the defenders pursued them, amidst smoke and fog, back towards the vines. Kienmayer tried yet again, this time with an additional three battalions of *grenzers*, driving the French back beyond the ditch to the refuge of the garden walls and houses. But if the *grenzers* alone could not achieve the objective, 3,000 reinforcements from the 1st Column soon arrived, driving up Allied numbers so high as to render the defence of Telnitz untenable. Having said this, the French were not prepared to abandon the place without offering further resistance. Somewhat rested by the hiatus between attacks and now reinforced with Russian light infantry provided by Buxhöwden, the assault resumed, now involving between 1,800 and 2,000 men (with another 1,000 in reserve), which led to fierce fighting in which the Allies finally ejected the fewer than 900 defenders from Telnitz, who retreated across the stream toward Sokolnitz, 1.25 miles (2km) to the north, on the west bank of the Goldbach.

At about 0830hrs, after over an hour and a half of fighting, the Allies stood in a position to advance against the French right and rear as Weyrother's plan stipulated. By this time they were aided by the fact that the fog was gradually clearing across most of the French line, apart from low-lying areas along the Goldbach. The Allied plan now required the 2nd Column, under General

Langeron, to approach the 1st Column's position in order to move forward together, with Langeron to proceed on a course through Sokolnitz and across the Goldbach. Yet while the Allies prepared to cross the brook at Telnitz, they suddenly came under unexpected attack themselves from reinforcements sent by Davout in the form of General Heudelet's Advance Guard, with the main body, Friant's division, close behind. Approaching from the west, Heudelet's men fixed bayonets amidst the thick fog, carefully avoided discharging their muskets and thus approached in virtual silence. Charging across the bridge south-west of the village, they entered Telnitz from the south, surprising Russian *jäger* who, not expecting a counter-attack – and certainly not from the south – fled. Having also driven out the Austrian *grenzers*, for the moment at least, the 15th Light and 108th Line held the village.

Austrian and Russian officers began to rally their fleeing troops, while Heudelet prepared for a counter-attack by deploying his troops in defensive positions in front of and inside the village. Standing in line in open ground between Telnitz and the vineyards, the 108th Line fell victim to a hussar attack on its flank, upon which the men broke and fled into the village, together with some of the 15th Light. The Allies followed up by occupying the ground in front of Telnitz and, with artillery brought up in support, began to bombard the French positions as Russian infantry approached from the north and east, engaging the 108th in the village streets and houses. Considerably outnumbered and weakened by heavy losses, after half an hour Heudelet withdrew to the north along the Goldbach and then across, harassed as he went by Allied artillery and cavalry following in his wake.

It was now about 0900hrs, with the fog lifting across the French positions. Notwithstanding increased visibility and their success in taking Telnitz, the Allies advanced cautiously, albeit reinforced with Russian infantry, assuming a position on high ground north-west of the village. Leaving the *grenzers* in Telnitz, Buxhöwden arrayed the rest of the 1st Column, consisting of twelve battalions, in an exposed area between Augezd and Telnitz. He now stood waiting, in accordance with Weyrother's plan, for Langeron's 2nd Column to the north to capture Sokolnitz, before the general Allied advance could proceed in parallel with all other columns. French resistance in Telnitz had delayed Buxhöwden, buying the French valuable time – time in which Napoleon could prepare his own advance.

Approximately 1.25 miles (2km) north of Telnitz lay the village of Sokolnitz, held by a detachment of about 350 *Tirailleurs du Po*, under Colonel Hulot. The remainder of the division under Legrand stood about 3 miles (5km) north, at Kobelnitz, where seven battalions of infantry were deployed. Just to the north of Sokolnitz stood a game park straddling the banks of the Goldbach, known as the pheasantry. Most of Hulot's men held an orchard, just east of the Goldbach, with others in the village and to the north in a series of stone structures forming Sokolnitz Castle – in fact more a country house than a proper fortification. Owing to a delay caused by the Allies forming up in the wrong positions, it was not until 0800hrs that Langeron's column began its advance toward the Goldbach, taking the road toward Klein Hostieradek to ease the steepness of the descent into the valley. The troops then proceeded through Augezd and followed the road to Sokolnitz. Thus, although the delay had cost the Allies half an hour, by 0830hrs the Russian general's column stood parallel with that of Kienmayer's, as planned. What had become of the 3rd Column – that of Prshibyshevsky, situated somewhere to the north and shrouded in fog – the other two commanders did not know.

Langeron, positioned facing the southern end of Sokolnitz, did not wish to assault the village without the co-operation of Prshibyshevsky, but in the absence of the latter commander's presence, Langeron proceeded to send forward his advance guard to engage the skirmishers thrown out by the French, while a battery of Russian artillery began to fire on the village. Meanwhile, Prshibyshevsky made his way toward Sokolnitz across ploughed fields and uneven ground, which slowed an advance that was further hindered when the frozen ground soon turned to mud.

Prshibyshevsky's 3rd Column finally reached a position to assist Langeron around 0900hrs, after a ninety-minute slog over a mere 2.5 miles (4km) of ground which choked the wheels of his guns with sticky mud.

The Russians enjoyed numerical superiority to an overwhelming degree, but Sokolnitz proved itself a formidably defensible place, with stone houses and walled gardens. The defenders, partly cloaked in fog and numbering no more than perhaps 500 divided between the village and the castle, held the Russians back with a magnificent fighting spirit. Meanwhile, two battalions of the 26th Light, en route to reinforce Telnitz from General Merle's brigade (3rd Division, Soult's IV Corps), reached Sokolnitz just as the firing began and took up positions in the streets, houses and the open ground between the village and the castle. Prshibyshevsky, his column ready for the attack, launched two battalions of Russian *jäger* across the Goldbach against the southern end of the village, while the main body of nine battalions stood by on the east bank of the stream. Further north, just after 0900hrs Sokolnitz Castle became the object of attention for two battalions of *jäger*, though other units from the 3rd Column would support, with a reserve to the north-east to block any French assistance arriving from Kobelnitz.

The outnumbered defenders in the castle rapidly abandoned the position, but as they followed up on open ground the *jäger* came under heavy fire from light infantry and artillery, causing them to retreat, thus enabling the French to re-occupy the castle. Further south, Russian infantry emerged through the fog, only to be repulsed with severe losses by accurate musket fire directed from the village. But the Russians, with the advantage of numbers, prepared to try again, now forewarned of French dispositions and possessed of an understanding of their opponents' strength. Langeron and Prshibyshevsky planned to use two battalions to seize the castle before assaulting the village, while three battalions would proceed between the castle and village, attacking the latter. Two more battalions of Russians would attack from the south, with other units in support and in reserve. In all, the Russians committed ten battalions to the attack with eight in support – all against two battalions of the 26th Light and the beleaguered *Tirailleurs du Po*.

The Russian attack began at 0930hrs, when *jäger* began to drive out skirmishers from the pheasantry while others struck the castle, obliging the defenders to abandon that position amidst fears of being surrounded by superior numbers. Russian infantry proceeded to occupy the open ground between the castle and the village, receiving heavy fire as they did so, and General Olsufiev's troops suffered heavy losses as they tried to seize a strong defensive position between the village and the brook. But the French could not hold out for long, for with five battalions attacking from the east, another three from the north, two more elsewhere and the capture of the French guns, the village inevitably fell, with the survivors retreating west in haste toward Turas. Their first objective taken at around 0945hrs, the Russians settled down to disentangle their units and reassemble the men in Sokolnitz amidst the fog and confusion of the recent fighting.

Pratzen Heights: The First Phase

2 December 1805		
	0800hrs	Soult's IV Corps begins its ascent of the Pratzen Heights
	0830hrs	Austro-Russian troops under Miloradovich and Kollowrath begin their march toward the village of Pratze
	0845hrs	Fierce engagements take place around the Pratzenberg and the Stare Vinohrady for possession of the Pratzen Heights; by 0930hrs the Allies risk being split in two

At dawn, about 0700hrs, eight French infantry divisions, plus a body of cavalry, stood in the valley of the Goldbach between Puntowitz and the Santon, a distance of about 3 miles (5km), ready to advance against the Pratzen Heights as stipulated in Napoleon's grand tactical plan. This disposition of forces left only one division

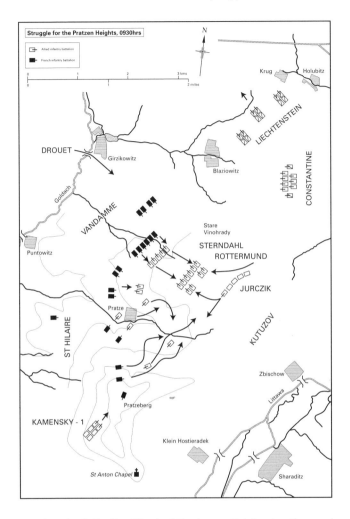

Struggle for the Pratzen Heights, 0930hrs

N

Allied infantry battalion
French infantry battalion

0   1   2   3 kms
0   1   2 miles

Krug   Holubitz

DROUET   Girzikowitz   Blaziowitz   LIECHTENSTEIN   CONSTANTINE

Goldbach

VANDAMME   Stare Vinohrady   STERNDAHL   ROTTERMUND

Puntowitz

JURCZIK

Pratze   KUTUZOV

ST HILAIRE   Zbischow

Littawa

Pratzeberg

KAMENSKY - 1   Klein Hostieradek

St Anton Chapel   Sharaditz

covering the 3.7 miles (6km) of the lower Goldbach – the weak deployment that the emperor had conceived in order to entice the Allies into concentrating their attacks in this sector. Napoleon's plan involved four divisions from IV and V Corps (Soult and Lannes, respectively) to advance in echelon. St Hilaire's division, near Puntowitz, would move first, with Vandamme's division on his left moving parallel from Girzikowitz. Once the two divisions of IV Corps had crossed the Goldbach, Bernadotte's I Corps would also cross the stream and position itself east of Girzikowitz, there to await further orders from the emperor. V Corps stood astride the Brünn–Olmütz road, with four cavalry divisions in support, while the Imperial Guard, established behind the Goldbach, would form part of the reserve, together with the combined grenadier division under Oudinot and two divisions of cuirassiers.

Meanwhile, the Allies had four columns assigned to the attack on the French right, some of whom had already begun to occupy positions on the lower Goldbach. Kutuzov sent the 4th Column (Miloradovich and Kollowrath) forward late, as its component elements took undue time to assemble. By 0730hrs, however, this combined Austro-Russian formation was proceeding toward the village of Pratze, with much of the Russian contingent moving along the road from Krenowitz and passing the Stare Vinohrady heights immediately to the east. The 4th Column proceeded with confidence, convinced that it could oust the French from Kobelnitz, while undertaking no reconnaissance to penetrate the fog to the west so as to ascertain French strength, dispositions or probable intention. There, the whole of the French forces arrayed between Kobelnitz in the south and the Santon in the north sat in silence, awaiting orders to advance from the emperor, who stood at his headquarters on Zuran Hill. Napoleon appreciated that his timing must be precise; specifically, to take possession of the heights only after the last elements of the 3rd Column could be seen passing Pratze and moving down the slope leading to Sokolnitz – and thus so that the whole Allied force reached the valley of the Goldbach, where the French intended to strike the fatal blow.

Shortly after the Allied columns were finally out of sight, Napoleon issued the order to advance, with the intention of using the divisions of St Hilaire and Vandamme (from Soult's IV Corps) to separate the Allied left and right by driving between them before attacking the southern half in the rear. Accordingly, the two divisions began moving at 0800hrs, ascending the heights from

*Marshal Nicolas Soult, commander of IV Corps. His divisions, under
St Hilaire and Vandamme, comprised some of the best in the army and
fought exceptionally well on the Pratzen Heights.*

the west, moving as quickly as possible toward the Pratzeberg –
the high point toward the southern section of the heights about
1,100 yards (1km) south of the village of Pratze. As the French
advanced they were detected by the Advance Guard under

General Wodniansky, his command established behind Pratze. The leading French elements and the Allied Advance Guard then rushed forward to reach the summit first, with the 10th Light succeeding. A French battalion then sought to occupy the village, only to discover Russian musketeers lining a ravine to the front of Pratze, from which they promptly repulsed the French attack. Thiébault's brigade renewed the challenge, this time routing the defenders holding a position in front of the village and seeking to envelop the place with the help of Vandamme's division.

The Russians sought to cobble together a defence against this entirely unexpected movement by the French, with Kutuzov ordering forward Repninsky's brigade, from Miloradovich's column, against opposing infantry on the Pratzeberg. More French forces appeared from amidst the fog as Kutuzov ordered Kollowrath to bring forward his division to oppose them. Both sides established firing positions and sought to drive the other off with exchanges of musket and artillery fire, with most of the fighting concentrated around the Stare Vinohrady, site of the tsar's headquarters, around the village of Pratze, and on the Pratzeberg, which commanded an impressive view of most of the battlefield. In quick order, twelve battalions of French infantry under St Hilaire and Vandamme became engaged with equal numbers of Russians under Miloradovich, but the fighting intensified as growing numbers of French troops appeared, raising their strength to over 12,000 – initially outnumbering the Allies' 5,000 Russian infantry and Austrian cavalry, but about equal in light of the 7,000 Austrian infantry advancing in support.

But numbers played little part in the action on the Pratzen Heights, for here, as elsewhere, the French demonstrated the superiority of their weapons handling, Thiébault recalling how at one point, seeking to inflict maximum damage on advancing Austrians, they:

> let the formidable masses approach within [40 yards] and then
> with my nine guns suddenly unmasked, the whole line poured
> in the most destructive fire ... Imagine my satisfaction when I

> saw each discharge cutting great square holes in the regiments
> … and these regiments … dispersing in fleeing masses.
>
> (Thiébault, *Mémoires*, vol. iii, pp. 471–72)

With volleys issued more rapidly and accurately than their opponents, and Russian and Austrian losses mounting near the Stare Vinohrady, the French drove some of their opponents back at bayonet point. Further south, overwhelmed by intense small arms and artillery fire, the Russians near the Pratzeberg fled, while others found themselves encircled in Pratze. It was not long before the Russian left collapsed, obliging the remainder of the line to give ground and so leaving the French in possession of the summit of the Pratzeberg and the village of Pratze. To the north, the French stood facing the Austrians with their right anchored against the Stare Vinohrady. Thus, in under an hour – with thirty to forty-five minutes of fighting and a short period for the French to ascend the Pratzen Heights – the action had reached a critical stage, with the Allies on the verge of being driven off the feature entirely and split in two.

Kutuzov, wounded by a musket ball but still in command and appreciating the crisis developing in his centre, urgently requested reinforcements from Prince Liechtenstein and Grand Duke Constantine, whose formations were situated to the north, there to aid the two Austrian brigades still on the heights. But Russian troops could not be spared, for the cavalry under the former was already committed to a fight further north against 17,000 infantry and cavalry under Lannes and Murat, whose respective commands, V Corps and the Cavalry Reserve, were then proceeding east via the Brünn–Olmütz road. A small number of Russians were, however, already on their way, having heard the firing on the heights; specifically, Kamensky I's reserve from the 2nd Column was en route from the south, but not yet even at Augezd. Moreover, with Liechtenstein's mixed Austro-Russian 5th Column about to engage a sizeable body of French between Blaziowitz and Krug, this left only Constantine's 10,600 elite troops in a position to serve as the reserve for an army now rent apart, with its 4th and 5th Columns no longer in direct contact.

Action in the Northern Sector

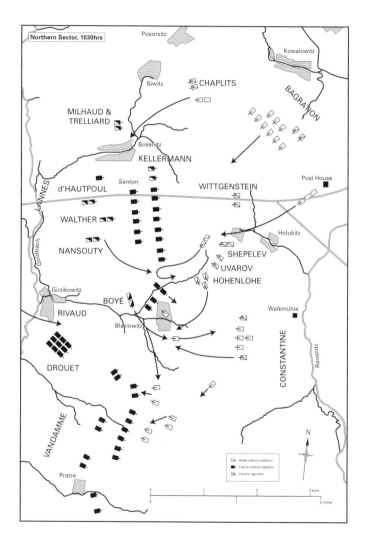

0830hrs	Liechtenstein (5th Column), with Hohenlohe's cavalry, establishes his troops in and around Blaziowitz; shortly thereafter, Bagration (Advance Guard) reaches a position between Kowalowitz and Slawikowitz, linking up with Kollowrath (4th Column)
0900hrs	Constantine's Russian Imperial Guard established on an elevated position just east of Blaziowitz; both sides move towards Blaziowitz in an attempt to occupy it first; the Russians succeed and set up defensive positions; fierce fighting ensues
0930hrs	Vandamme's and Drouet's divisions (from IV and I Corps, respectively) cross the Goldbach, followed by Rivaud's (from I Corps)
1000hrs	Bernadotte's I Corps advances from Girzikowitz and up the Pratzen Heights; Constantine orders the Imperial Guard to move against Blaziowitz to try to prevent a wedge developing in Allied lines; intense fighting follows
1030hrs	Under pressure from overwhelming numbers, the Russians withdraw from Blaziowitz
1100hrs	Finding himself unable to oust the French from Blaziowitz, Bagration concentrates on seizing Bosenitz, which falls, only to be retaken by a French counter-attack
1130hrs	Constantine plugs the gap left by the retreating Russians
1230hrs	Constantine's troops disengage from the action around Blaziowitz and proceed toward Krenowitz; Lannes' V Corps advances against the villages of Krug and Holubitz, while other elements march on Blaziowitz

While the French had achieved considerable success on the Pratzen Heights, to the north opposition to Lannes was beginning to require a change to the emperor's original intention of forcing the Allies south. Earlier in the morning Liechtenstein had moved his column to the vicinity of the village of Blaziowitz, as his instructions required, there to form a connection between Kollowrath's 4th Column and Bagration's Advance Guard along the Brünn–Olmütz road. By 0830hrs Count Hohenlohe had established his troops near Blaziowitz, while to Liechtenstein's rear Bagration deployed his men for the purpose of anchoring the right flank of the army. Once Bagration reached his position between Kowalowitz and Slawikowitz, he was to remain there until the 4th Column had advanced beyond Kobelnitz, after which Bagration was to proceed against the French left. Also in the north stood Constantine's superbly disciplined units of the Russian Imperial Guard, which at around 0900hrs established itself on an elevated position just east of Blaziowitz. Thus, three major components of the Allied army, composing the right wing, operated in the northern sector: the 5th Column (Liechtenstein), the Advance Guard (Bagration) and the Russian Imperial Guard (Constantine).

Opposing them stood at least four French infantry divisions, four heavy cavalry divisions and eight regiments of light cavalry in support. These stood between Girzikowitz and the Santon, where either Napoleon could unleash them against the Allies at the vital moment or they could hold the French line in the north if the Allies launched a general attack in that sector. Vandamme's and Drouet's divisions crossed the river by 0930hrs, followed by Rivaud's, which reached the other side an hour later. Lannes was to advance up the Brünn–Olmütz road once he could perceive St Hilaire's men on the Pratzeberg. This occurred at about 0915hrs, and Lannes moved into the open ground between Bosenitz and Blaziowitz. This prompted action from all three Allied column commanders, above all at 0930hrs when cavalry from Liechtenstein's column charged Kellermann's horsemen – almost 1,400 *uhlans* against about 1,300 French cavalry. Kellermann's troopers retreated amidst the gaps between accompanying infantry columns, pursued by the Russians. They, in turn, found themselves disorganised and under very close-range fire as their lancers, practically stationary from the exhausting effort of the charge, prodded at the infantry with little effect. Kellermann then reformed his regiments and charged the *uhlans* before they could reconstitute into a proper formation.

The French captured many, but most of the lancers escaped through gaps in the ranks of opposing infantry, leaving behind over 200 killed, severely wounded or captured. A whole series of

Marshal Joachim Murat, the most remarkable cavalry commander of his age, served with distinction in the Austerlitz campaign, as well as later in Prussia, Poland, Spain, Russia and Germany.

mounted clashes followed when Russian hussars led by Uvarov counter-attacked, sparking off a general mêlée involving hundreds of light cavalry engaged in furious action before the Russians eventually withdrew south.

At around 0900hrs, just prior to the cavalry clash, both sides came to the realisation that they must occupy Blaziowitz; the French so that they could profit from the gaps already created in the Allied line, and the Allies to deny the French the ability to drive a wedge between their right and centre. Accordingly, Russian Guard *jäger* and some guns were sent to occupy the village, while at the same time, Lannes was approaching Blaziowitz from the Brünn–Olmütz road, extending lines of skirmishers ahead of his main body to try to reach the village first. In the event, the Russians achieved their aim and took up defensive positions in the houses and gardens, repulsing the French who arrived immediately in their wake. A vicious engagement now ensued, with the Russian commander, St Priest, requesting immediate reinforcements from Constantine, who sent him only a single battalion. Another was detached to Kutuzov who, then struggling to keep possession of the Pratzen Heights, had also requested support. But St Priest required more than a token gesture, for as more French infantry approached Blaziowitz at around 1030hrs, they possessed sufficient numbers to encircle it. Realising that he could not hope to hold his position against the superior numbers soon to envelop him, St Priest withdrew his *jäger* and reached the safety of Constantine's lines. The French promptly occupied the village, having taken 300 prisoners and five guns.

At the same time, while Bernadotte's troops were on the move from Girzikowitz, Austrian cavalry attacked, albeit against such a large body of infantry that they could register no appreciable impact and were obliged to retire. While they managed to delay the infantry's progress by half an hour, the Austrians' efforts failed to aid their comrades on the western edge of the heights, from which they were forced to withdraw. Bernadotte now continued his progress up the heights, while Constantine, anxious to prevent

Marshal Jean Lannes, commander of V Corps at Austerlitz. He was to have spearheaded the wide flanking movement Napoleon planned against the Allied right flank, but unexpectedly heavy fighting in the northern sector rendered this impossible.

a wedge developing and dividing the army in two, ordered the Imperial Guard to advance on Blaziowitz, where it could help plug the gap and assist the 4th Column's flank. Accordingly, four battalions of Russian guard infantry launched a bayonet attack which, notwithstanding heavy French fire, drove back the first three battalions they encountered before halting in front of a second line of French infantry. Of these the guardsmen intended to make short work; however, before they could proceed they received instructions to abandon their positions, for Kutuzov wanted the heights cleared of Allied troops as part of a general withdrawal, with the focus of battle to fall on the southern sector. By about 1230hrs, Constantine's forces had disengaged from the action, formed up in columns and proceeded toward Krenowitz.

Elsewhere, but also in the vicinity of the Brünn–Olmütz road, a number of cavalry combats took place, most notably involving General Nansouty's eighteen squadrons of cuirassiers and carabiniers against ten squadrons of Russian hussars, in which the latter were routed and pursued to the Holubitz brook, behind which the broken light cavalry found refuge. Fresh Russian troopers, however, pursued the French heavy cavalry as it withdrew, though in encountering opposing infantry and, having lost momentum, the Russians found themselves shot down in large numbers before making their retreat. Several other charges and counter-charges followed, with the Russians finally retreating across the Rausnitz brook to lick their wounds and leaving empty behind them the sizeable area between Holubitz and Blaziowitz – a space which French infantry under Rivaud hoped to fill. Constantine undertook to prevent this, and at about 1130hrs, with the area clear of cavalry, sent his column forward for this purpose.

With the Russians unable to drive the French from Blaziowitz, at about 1100hrs Bagration turned his attention on Bosenitz, an attack upon which could offer a diversion from the French effort further south. Only a small detachment held Bosenitz and the Russian *jäger* sent to seize the place experienced no difficulty in driving out the tiny garrison and pursuing it in the direction of the Santon until artillery forced the attackers to fall back to the village. Finding his flank now exposed by the capture of Bosenitz, Lannes ordered Claparède to recapture the place, for Lannes did not want to continue his advance with an enemy to his rear. Infantry, supported by cavalry, duly left their defensive positions on the Santon and stormed the village, where only brief fighting took place before the *jäger* abandoned the place to forces which outnumbered them many times over.

In all, the Allies had precipitated numerous infantry and cavalry engagements, but with no attempt at co-ordination, probably because they did not expect a general French advance in the northern sector of the battlefield. Having said this, if the fighting that raged between Blaziowitz and Bosenitz had any effect, it was to delay the French and provide time for the Allies to consolidate many of their scattered forces – ultimately an important factor in the preservation of this wing of the Allied army in light of the disasters which were to befall most of the rest of it. The cost was high on both sides, but particularly for the Russians; yet they succeeded through notable aggressiveness in denying Napoleon the ability to execute his plans as originally intended. But if the emperor thus found himself obliged to abandon the idea of turning the Allied right flank, even with Blaziowitz in his possession, a new opportunity now presented itself to him, for affairs on the Pratzen Heights were turning very much in Napoleon's favour.

Pratzen Heights: The Second Phase

2 December 1805		
	1000hrs	With fighting continuing on the Heights, Kutuzov reinforces the beleaguered units there with the Austrian contingent from 4th Column (Miloradovich and Kollowrath)
	1100hrs	Austrians around the Stare Vinohrady under Kollowrath withdraw; fighting continues around the Pratzenberg before the Allies flee toward Krenowtiz and Zbischow
	1230hrs	Last Allied resistance on the Pratzen Heights

At 1000hrs the Austrian line on the Pratzen, its right wing anchored on the Stare Vinohrady, continued to hold, while beleaguered Russians still continued to contest possession of the Pratzeberg. By odd circumstances, the opposing forces in the two remaining contested areas of the Pratzen Heights faced one another with mismatched numbers: in the north, Vandamme deployed 7,000 men against about 5,000 Austrians around the Stare Vinohrady, while in the south St Hilaire's 4,500 men held the Pratzeberg against about 4,000 Allied troops. On the outcome of the fighting in these two sectors rested the fortunes of the Allied army, for these two elements of Allied forces crucially constituted the only units preventing the French from dividing the army in half.

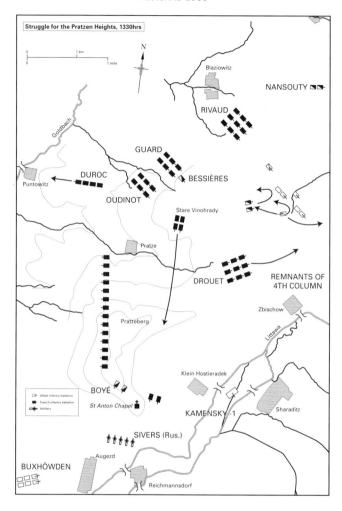

Struggle for the Pratzen Heights, 1330hrs

Accordingly, Kutuzov now sent the Austrian contingent in the 4th Column – eight battalions for deployment and seven in reserve – to confront the twenty French battalions under St Hilaire and Vandamme. Having ascended the heights, they drew up in lines while Miloradovich's Russians tried to reform in anticipation of a French assault. A general engagement soon followed, and Kollowrath's Austrians were arriving just as the Allied effort on the heights was about to collapse; much therefore hinged on their conduct. Other Allied units, in fact, were already en route, including Kamensky with two regiments returning to the Pratzeberg, from where they had only recently departed. St Hilaire, around the tiny village of Pratze, deployed his 4,000 men in line in the open to face Kamensky's 2,500 men, while Vandamme, situated further north, ordered an attack on the Austrians which drove them back near the Stare Vinohrady. Nonetheless, the French met stiff resistance and crumbled before a bayonet counter-attack, with the jubilant Austrians themselves seen off almost immediately in disorderly fashion by French dragoons. Still, Austrian resistance afforded precious time with which the Russians could recover from their earlier drubbing. Nine battalions managed to reform themselves behind the Austrians, while Kollowrath maintained his lines and sensibly kept a number of battalions in reserve.

Near the Pratzeberg, fighting developed as Kamensky's infantry appeared on the scene, to be met by accurate musket fire from the light infantry defending this position. Two hours' fighting left half the Russians' two regiments strewn on the ground dead or wounded, as the Russian general, Langeron, recorded:

Soon, the French lines initiated a very sharp and very murderous fire of musket and canister upon the brigade of Kamensky which in a moment had many men rendered *hors de combat*. [Kamensky's brigade] answered with a less sharp and badly directed fire; the majority of our soldiers fired in the air… in justice I ought to say that despite the critical situation they found themselves in, despite the superior number of the enemy, despite their little experience of war and the effect on them of an unforeseen attack on their rear, despite the noise of gunfire, which many of them were hearing for the first time, they maintained themselves admirably for nearly two hours …

(Langeron, *Journal Inédit*, p. 75)

Meanwhile, slightly to the north, near Pratze but extending to the Pratzeberg, Jurczik's Austrian brigade advanced against Thiébault's position, where the French infantry were instructed to hold their fire until the attackers had nearly reached their position. Having unleashed a destructive volley, a masked battery suddenly appeared as the ranks opened up, tearing rounds through the already stunned Austrians and stalling the attack. Having seized back the initiative, Thiébault ordered his infantry to counter-attack in what developed into a sustained fire fight.

Meanwhile, to the north, Vandamme vigorously prosecuted his attacks in the vicinity of the Stare Vinohrady, with Ferey's brigade of six battalions, at around 1030hrs, moving against the Austrian left, while Brigadier Schiner sought to attack from the north, engaging their right with the bayonet. At about the same time, on the Pratzeberg, Kamensky's Russians were beginning to lose the fire fight that had been raging for the previous twenty minutes, while their Austrian comrades on their right were also faltering. Appreciating that his men could not match the French in musketry, Kamensky opted to charge, his men almost reaching the summit of the Pratzeberg before the more numerous French obliged them to retreat. Shortly thereafter, at around 1100hrs, after about an hour of severe fighting, the Austrians of Kollowrath's command streamed away from the area around the Stare Vinohrady and sought refuge behind the Allied second line of Austrians and Russians. The strength of the French onslaught having already accounted for many prisoners and some captured Allied artillery, Kollowrath felt obliged to order the whole of the line in that sector to withdraw, abandoning to the French one of the two key positions on the heights.

Kutuzov, meanwhile, remained undaunted about the fall of the Stare Vinohrady, and ordered a renewed attack on the Pratzeberg, hoping at least to avert disaster to the Allies by retaking the position to his front and denying the French control of the whole plateau. Austrian and Russian infantry charged ahead with the bayonet, only to be driven back by intense fire and losing General

Jurczik, who fell mortally wounded. Further attacks met the same fate, leaving hundreds of the attackers littering the ground. Amidst this stalemate, Langeron ordered Kamensky to hold the line, while the former left in search of reinforcements from the 1st Column, then at Telnitz.

After two hours of intense fighting, in the course of which he drove off Kollowrath's forces and prevented the Allies from retaking the Pratzeberg, Napoleon had completed the first phase of his plan, albeit after suffering heavy casualties. Nevertheless, far greater casualties were inflicted on the Austro-Russian forces, who, when the French attacked, appeared in greater force on the Pratzen Heights than the emperor had expected. Success on the Heights allowed Napoleon to initiate the second phase of his plan, involving most of his reserve: two divisions from I Corps as well as the Imperial Guard, who were ordered to advance. Rivaud's division proceeded toward Blaziowitz; Drouet, on his right, moved to reinforce St Hilaire's division; and the Imperial Guard and the Reserve Grenadiers under Oudinot left Zuran Hill and proceeded to cross the Goldbach. Napoleon and his staff thereupon decamped, with the intention of establishing headquarters on the newly captured Stare Vinohrady, which offered perspective over the whole of the heights.

The last Allied resistance on the heights occurred between 1115hrs and 1130hrs, when Vandamme attacked Austrian and Russian elements in the Allies' third line of defence, which quickly collapsed, the disordered fugitives making for Krenowitz and Zbischow. Drouet's division reached the western edge of the heights shortly thereafter. The last remnants of the 4th Column on the heights, Kamensky's brigade, faced envelopment at around 1230hrs after brief fighting and ran off toward Klein Hostieradek. With the French in control of the heights by midday, the climax of the battle was over, the Allies having offered a remarkable degree of resistance over the course of nearly three hours. In the end, superior French training, discipline and skill at arms had told.

Renewed Fighting in the Southern Sector

| 2 December 1805 | 1030hrs | Friant's division counter-attacks the Russians in front of Sokolnitz, in the course of which the village changes hands several times; reinforcements arrive from Davout at 1100hrs |
| | 1200hrs | Fighting around Sokolnitz ceases, with the Russians still in possession there and in Telnitz; French forces fall back to the heights overlooking Sokolnitz; for the next thirty minutes both sides regroup for a renewal of fighting |

While savage fighting had raged on the Pratzen Heights between 0900hrs and noon, to the south Buxhöwden and Prshibyshevsky, leading the 2nd and 3rd Columns, respectively, continued to adhere to the Allied plan, seeking to push further west from Sokolnitz. By 0930hrs these forces had duly taken Sokolnitz and crossed the Goldbach, but French resistance prevented them from proceeding in the direction of Turas, in tandem with the 1st Column, operating to the south. Worse, while the Russians engaged in regrouping and reorganising their forces in the wake of the capture of Sokolnitz, word arrived of developments on the Pratzen Heights. This constituted disconcerting news in its own right, but Langeron and Olsufiev had foolishly assumed that, having driven the French out of Sokolnitz, their opponents were not in a position to counter-attack; indeed, that they were in full retreat. This was not the case, and by allowing their men to reform in open ground to the west of the village for half an hour rather than withdraw them to the protection of the village, Langeron and Olsufiev had left their men vulnerable. Prshibyshevsky at least had the sense to shift his men closer to the village and the castle, even as French artillery fire began to play on the Russians and Friant advanced from the west with a fresh division.

Although outnumbered, Friant enjoyed the element of surprise and pressed home his attack, striking principally from the south. There the Russians showed themselves ill prepared to receive an assault and the infantry of the 48th Line descended and drove them out of the houses – though neither cheaply nor without the Russians offering a spirited fighting retreat. At 1030hrs the 111th Line entered the fray, driving Russian infantry into the village from the west. At the northern end of Sokolnitz the Russians also offered stiff resistance, and with reinforcements ordered forward by Olsufiev, the Russians drove out the 111th Line. Thereafter, the village changed hands at least twice in the ensuing mêlée, with much of the fighting occurring in the open ground between the village and Sokolnitz Castle, combined with heavy skirmish fire around the pheasantry – all places already choked with the dead and dying from the fighting earlier that morning. This to-and-fro carnage carried on for an hour, forestalling the intended Allied advance across the Goldbach.

At about 1100hrs, however, the see-saw nature of the fighting altered with the arrival of another brigade of Friant's division, which flung itself against the Russians clinging desperately to the north-western end of the village. Friant's men drove the green-coated defenders back inside, before following up their success and engaging in further, bitter house-to-house fighting in the course of which the Russians managed to retake possession of the village by about midday. Each side then reformed, awaiting a renewal of the blood-letting.

Thus, after two hours of intense fighting, the French, despite inferior numbers, had prevented the Allies from regaining the initiative in this sector and held most of the heights overlooking the Goldbach. The battered Allies, for their herculean efforts, held the village and Castle and the area immediately to the west. Oddly, while Prshibyshevsky and Buxhöwden continued to prosecute the offensive in the south as directed, no one informed them of the full extent of the disaster befalling their comrades on the Pratzen Heights. As such, while Kutuzov was ordering the withdrawal of all troops from that feature toward Austerlitz and Krenowitz, he failed to appreciate the danger to which he was exposing his left wing around Telnitz and Sokolnitz.

The Guards in Contention

1300hrs	Attack of the Russian Imperial Guard on the Pratzen Heights
1315hrs	French troops begin descending the Heights just north of Augezd
1500hrs	Attack of the Russian Imperial Guard decisively defeated, leaving the Allied army split in half; entire plain between Bosenitz and Posorsitz free of Russian troops after two hours of intense fighting

The morning's fighting had resulted in the French defeating the Allied army and consequently obliging Kutuzov to order its general withdrawal. Nevertheless, owing to the unexpectedly fierce resistance encountered in the northern sector, Napoleon could not, by the afternoon, hope to drive the whole of the Allied army into the ponds and swamps to the south as he had envisaged. However, having split Kutuzov's force in the centre, he could conceivably carry out his original plan on a smaller scale, particularly by engaging his uncommitted reserves. To start, the divisions of Vandamme and St Hilaire would attack southward in a great wheeling movement while, to the north, Bernadotte's I Corps would hold the Pratzen Heights and protect the right flank of Lannes's corps proceeding up the Brünn–Olmütz road.

While Napoleon refined his plan, the Allies struggled with the extreme difficulties of extricating their forces from the field, for even while those troops on the Pratzen Heights were shifting east, thirty-seven battalions and a small body of Austrian cavalry remained around Telnitz and Sokolnitz, thirteen battalions of which stood on the west side of the Goldbach. These were about to come under pressure from – amongst other formations intending to converge on the southern sector – most of the troops now on the Pratzen Heights under Vandamme and St Hilaire, plus nine more battalions under Drouet from Bernadotte's corps, the whole of which was poised to move south. Thus began the next phase of the battle, in which the Allied reserve, more by accident than design, entered the fray as Kutuzov's tactical options rapidly drained away.

The timing was not fortuitous, for Kutuzov's decision came while Constantine's troops of the Russian Imperial Guard were in the process of withdrawing towards Krenowitz in the wake of their brief success earlier in the day near Blaziowitz. In the course of their movement to this effect, they encountered French infantry on the Pratzen Heights to the right of their route of withdrawal: some east of the Stare Vinohrady facing Krenowitz and others just south facing Zbischow. No sooner had a battalion been sent forward by Vandamme to identify the approaching column, than Russian cavalry burst upon the 24th Light, which formed square, while the Life Guard Horse attacked a battalion of the 4th Line, which also formed square, repelling the cavalry with heavy musket fire as the horsemen swirled around its sides. The infantry suffered heavy casualties, however, from supporting Russian horse artillery, which fired canister shot – a form of anti-personnel ammunition which showered its target with musket balls like a giant shotgun – into their densely packed ranks, leaving a gaping hole into which the Life Guard Horse funnelled, breaking the square and capturing the 4th Line's precious imperial eagle. More cavalry attacked, this time to clear other French infantry from the route Constantine required for his progress to Krenowitz. The Life Guard Horse, having re-formed from its previous charge, struck the left flank of the 24th Light, which was foolishly arrayed in line, while the Life Guard Hussars charged their right. Both flanks now assailed, the infantry broke and fled, abandoning their eagle in the dirt. Although the actions between the Russian cavalry and French infantry went unseen at Napoleon's headquarters on the Stare Vinohrady, owing to the folds in the ground which limited visibility, when men of the 4th Line and 24th Light routed practically into the midst of the emperor's entourage, the extent of the setback revealed itself. Remaining nevertheless unperturbed, the emperor called up the cavalry of the Imperial Guard to rectify the situation.

Marshal Bessières stood with these impressive regiments near the Stare Vinohrady, where he deployed the *Chasseurs à Cheval*, the Mamelukes and the *Grenadiers à Cheval* in three lines. At the same time, the Russian guard cavalry was in the process of re-assembling after chasing off the French infantry. While still stationary, the Life Guard Hussars received the *Chasseurs à Cheval*, themselves moving at only a trot at this stage. Already weakened by several rounds of fire from French horse artillery into their flank, the hussars ran off in a rout, leaving the path free for Bessières' cavalry to descend upon the Russian guard infantry marching toward Krenowitz. The Preobrazhensky Guard reached the vineyard, obviating the need to form square, but the Semenovsky Regiment, standing on open ground, had no choice but to do so, driving off the attack, with support from artillery and little damage to its ranks.

The repulse, however, proved only temporary. Constantine redoubled his efforts to move his column along its route, with one battalion reaching Krenowitz around 1400hrs but the remainder coming under skirmish fire before finally reaching the safety of the village. Much of the infantry of the Russian Imperial Guard then proceeded busily to cross the Rausnitz stream, much of this in a confused manner. Drouet's infantry and the guard cavalry duly followed up and reached the area, enabling the latter to attack (albeit unsuccessfully) two battalions of the Semenovsky Guard, who formed square and easily saw off the hostile cavalry, but failed to receive any support from the reserve artillery, many of whose guns were lost in the withdrawal. A third square, however, broke at the hands of the Mamelukes, who saw the fugitives off toward Krenowitz and captured a few prisoners as well as the battalion standard.

The defeat of the Semenovsky Guard and the gap left in the line by their rout obliged the remaining infantry units of the Russian Imperial Guard to withdraw down the slope, pursued by skirmishers from Drouet's and Rivaud's divisions. Just after 1400hrs, Constantine called upon Maliutin on the heights

Marshal Jean Baptiste Bessières, commander of the French Imperial Guard cavalry, which briefly engaged their Russian counterparts on the Pratzen Heights.

overlooking Krenowitz to march immediately to his aid, to help cover the withdrawal of the Russian Imperial Guard infantry and artillery still on the opposite bank of the Rausnitz. Maliutin's command consisted of the Chevalier Guard and the Life Guard Cossacks, seven squadrons in all, which crossed the stream and

The Chevalier Guard in action on the Pratzen Heights.

passed uneasily through the ranks of some of the retreating infantry. They then proceeded to attack French skirmishers in advance of the main body before carrying on into, and driving off, French light cavalry engaged in harassing the retreating Russian infantry and guns. In the course of this, the Chevalier Guard and Life Guard Cossacks saw before them at the top of the slope, running up from the stream, the whole of Drouet's division and part of Rivaud's, as well as the French *Chasseurs* and Mamelukes who, tired from their previous engagement, fell back. A second line of Imperial Guard cavalry, however, including part of the *Grenadiers à Cheval*, began to surround their opponents. Just before 1500hrs, this course attracted the remaining squadrons of the Chevalier Guard, the *Grenadiers à Cheval* and other squadrons from both sides to engage one another in a frenzied mêlée. As in so many other mounted engagements at Austerlitz, the Russians were left retreating, in this case toward Krenowitz, with losses to their Imperial Guard numbering about 300 cavalry, plus 600 infantry and artillery. Including the wounded, total losses sustained by Constantine's formation probably numbered over 1,500 men. By contrast, the French fared much better: fewer than 150 killed and several times that number wounded.

The defeat of the Russian Imperial Guard confirmed the division of the Allied army into two parts, with one final stage remaining in the battle during which Napoleon could proceed with his plan to drive the Allied columns in the south to their doom – though events in the north first require some comment.

Final Phases

	1230hrs	On the southern sector, Buxhöwden, commander of the Allied left wing, receives an order from Kutuzov for a general withdrawal, but fails to implement it for about an hour; Davout, seeking to recover lost ground, attacks Sokolnitz, resulting in two and a half hours of vicious fighting; Langeron, now aware of the Allies' crisis on the Pratzen Heights, orders a withdrawal to the east side of the Goldbach; on the northern sector, Lannes' V Corps advances against the villages of Krug and Holubitz; Suchet moves against Siwitz, obliging Russian withdrawal
2 December 1805	**1315hrs**	In the centre, St Hilaire's division begins descent from the Pratzen Heights to Sokolonitz; other French formations appear just north of Augezd

1400hrs	Having cleared Krug in the north, the French drive out the Russians from Holubitz
1415hrs	Principal French attack commences against Bagration's main line and quickly drives it back in disorder toward Kowalowitz and beyond; by 1430hrs virtually all Russians from the 3rd and 4th Columns west of the Goldbach now either *hors de combat* or driven east across the stream
1500hrs	Assailed by overwhelming numbers, the Russians flee from Sokolnitz, leaving many surrounded; the French follow up toward Telnitz; fugitives of 3rd Column desperately seek to escape encirclement, with many killed or captured; between 12,000 and 14,000 Allied troops now hemmed in on the southern sector, with a limited avenue of retreat
1530hrs	Effective co-ordinated resistance by Allied forces ceases; troops in full retreat
1600hrs	Fleeing Allied troops cross the frozen Satchan Pond, their combined weight, in conjunction with French artillery fire, breaking the ice and causing panic but little loss of life

By 1230hrs, once Constantine had begun his retreat from Blaziowitz and other formations had left the vicinity of Bosenitz in the north, the French could once again pursue Napoleon's plan to turn the Allied right and force it southward. This enterprise, which was to have involved fighting along the Brünn–Olmütz road, began, however, to go awry when the Allies sought first, as we have seen, to hold the Pratzen Heights and later, once driven off, to retake them. Nevertheless, Lannes, whose corps stood in the northern sector, was eager to attack Bagration, irrespective of developments elsewhere on the field. Part of V Corps' infantry advanced against the villages of Krug and Holubitz, while other elements moved toward Blaziowitz, already in French hands, thereby freeing up those troops to proceed with the others already destined for the assault against Krug and Holubitz. Bagration had taken advantage of the cavalry action to deploy his infantry with care in anticipation of eventual attack. His deployment – his left behind the Holubitz ravine and his right on the heights near Siwitz – placed him in a position which facilitated retreat and the possibility of establishing a second line of defence. Opposing forces roughly amounted to fifteen Russian battalions, forty-three squadrons of

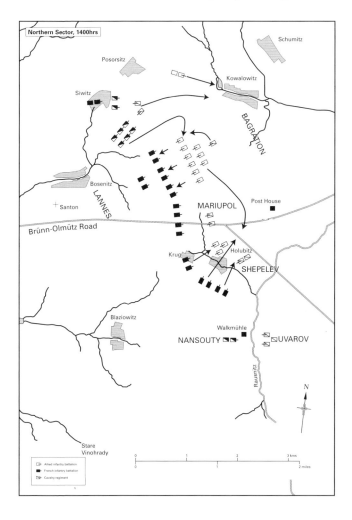

regular cavalry and between twenty and thirty of Cossacks, plus fifty-three guns. The French, under Lannes and Murat, mustered together twenty battalions, seventy-two squadrons and about thirty-two guns. Most of these units had not yet been engaged in the day's combat and were eager for the fight. As the ground did not favour a flanking manoeuvre, Lannes opted to attack frontally, with the main effort against Krug and Holubitz.

The French advance began at about 1230hrs, with contact made about fifteen minutes later at Krug, where the heavily outnumbered garrison was ordered back to the Allied main position behind the Holubitz stream. Holubitz itself, in turn, came under attack, though the Russians repulsed it with canister fire. At the same time, further north, Suchet moved against Siwitz, obliging the Russians there to withdraw to Posorsitz, just short of which some hapless *jäger* sustained casualties at the hands of cuirassiers before reaching Kowalowitz, together with other infantry which had managed to form square.

The principal French attack, however, began at around 1415hrs, when, after preparatory artillery fire, Suchet advanced his infantry against Bagration's main line, only to be repulsed with severe losses from Russian musket and artillery fire, which left Suchet himself wounded. The French regrouped and prepared to renew their assault, while Murat busily assembled his cavalry for a large-scale engagement against the Russian cavalry in this sector. With Krug and Holubitz behind them, the French now faced the Russian line deployed south-west of the Posorsitz Post House, with the Rausnitz stream to their left. Suchet duly attacked the centre of the Russian line, supported by Murat's cavalry. The infantry – six battalions with bayonets fixed – came under heavy fire, while Murat's troopers strode forward, dragoons and cuirassiers outflanking the Russian hussars to their front and driving them and a body of Cossacks off toward Kowalowitz. The infantry, meanwhile, bore the fire offered them and broke the Russian line, causing heavy losses and leaving the centre and right of Bagration's line in tatters by 1430hrs. The fleeing Russians made their way toward Kowalowitz and the main road, and after further brief resistance overcome by a cuirassier attack against the rear of some of their infantry, the Russians abandoned the whole area between Bosenitz and the Posorsitz Post House to French hands.

To the south, in the valley of the Goldbach, the Allied forces there, the 2nd and 3rd Columns, remained without new orders in spite of the retreat from the Pratzen Heights at around 1230hrs. For their part, Prshibyshevsky and Olsufiev did not want to pursue their offensive any further – and yet had no orders from Buxhöwden to withdraw. Davout, however, wished to recover lost ground, and at about 1230hrs attacked Sokolnitz with a view to repossessing it. Langeron, now aware of the Allied predicament on the Pratzen Heights, at the same time ordered a withdrawal to the east side of the Goldbach, where he could prepare a counter-attack against the French right in that sector, consisting of St Hilaire's division. Accordingly, about 3,000 Russians proceeded with the intention of assisting Kamensky. As these advanced, the remaining Russian infantry around Sokolnitz came under attack from Davout's corps, and for the next two and half hours fierce and confused fighting took place along the entire length of front, from the pheasantry to the southern end of Sokolnitz. Involving about 4,500 men on each side, the specific sequence of fighting is not known, but the Russians clearly put up stubborn resistance, with much close combat in the streets and houses. As the Russian left eventually caved in, Prshibyshevsky's men found themselves isolated near Sokolnitz Castle with only a single bridge over the Goldbach as an avenue of escape, while other battalions, cut off in the south of the village, clung on, contesting the occupation of every house. Intense fighting in and around Sokolnitz continued until the events on the Pratzen Heights began to have an impact on this sector, when victorious French forces moved south from Kobelnitz and approached Sokolnitz from the east.

Between 1315hrs and 1330hrs, St Hilaire's division began its advance down the slope to Sokolnitz, with spirits high as a consequence of the troops' triumph on the Pratzen Heights.

While Buxhöwden stood virtually paralysed and behaving oddly, and with Langeron seeing his rear threatened, the latter commander began withdrawing south what forces he could. Meanwhile, more French units reached the pheasantry and opposed approximately equal numbers of defenders, but by attacking the Russian right flank the French obliged their retreat, some struggling across the stream and others fleeing south, hoping to re-join the 1st Column. It was now impossible for the Russians to hold the line of the Goldbach, being engaged simultaneously from the west, north and the east, rendering retreat the only sensible option. Many were cut off, such as those in Sokolnitz Castle, which became a scene of desperate resistance. The Russians, overwhelmed, simply could not stand, and the place duly fell, together with the village itself, with many defenders trapped by the onslaught directed from both sides of the Goldbach. The fighting in and around Sokolnitz largely faded away at about 1500hrs, with the 2nd and 3rd Columns of the Allied army either killed, captured, lying wounded on the field or in scattered retreat. The French accordingly continued south toward Telnitz.

There, north-west of the village, the forces of Dokhturov and Kienmayer (sixteen battalions and twenty squadrons) stood on the west side of the Goldbach stream with the village to their rear; the French troops they had defeated earlier that morning faced them – about five and a half battalions and eighteen squadrons. Other units, perhaps twelve battalions, occupied the area around Augezd, forming the 1st Column's reserve. Most of these forces should not have been present at all, for while Buxhöwden had received Kutuzov's orders for a general withdrawal shortly after 1230hrs, he had not acted upon them. Indeed, he remained static until Langeron arrived at his headquarters perhaps an hour later to underscore the critical predicament of the Allies. When he did finally issue orders for retreat to Kienmayer and Dokhturov, they were directed to re-cross the Goldbach and proceed along the narrow causeway which stretched between the Satchan and

Mönitz ponds. Buxhöwden's reserve would march via Augezd and cross the River Littawa, to rendezvous later with the remains of the 4th Column.

Critically, by neglecting to issue orders for a general withdrawal in a timely manner, Buxhöwden failed to ensure the escape of much of the Allied army. Kienmayer and Dokhturov did indeed begin to withdraw, but at around 1315hrs French troops started descending the heights just north of Augezd, with the intention of pursuing the retreating Allies in the direction of the village of that name – though some French forces drove Allied units into Telnitz and out the other side, causing them to stream eastwards. Be that as it may, by 1500hrs, the French had hemmed in between 12,000 and 14,000 Allied troops, some with access to the bridge across the Littwa at Reichmannsdorf as a means of retreat, but most confined to the narrow causeways west of the Satchan pond or obliged to cross the frozen ice covering it. Needless to say, the French did not simply allow the Allies to retreat unhindered, and

Retreating Russian troops breaking through the ice covering the Satchan pond. Napoleon claimed 20,000 Russian soldiers drowned here, but in fact probably no more than 200 perished in admittedly freezing, but very shallow, water. About 20 guns and 150 horses were also lost.

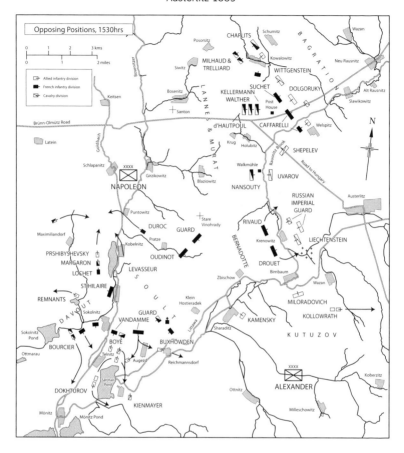

thus, following them up, they quickly seized Augezd and placed artillery on the heights overlooking that village. Further west, as Allied forces funnelled through the narrow passage between the Satchan and Mönitz ponds, many fugitives took a path across the frozen ice of the Satchan pond when one of the causeways over the Littawa collapsed from the weight of artillery. French artillery fire deliberately directed against the ice, together with the weight of men, horses and guns, soon broke it, sending scores into the freezing water, together with the guns and their horse teams –

General Rapp presenting Austrian and Russian prisoners and standards to the emperor.

though not on the epic scale of thousands, as Napoleon would later claim in one of his characteristically exaggerated bulletins. At the same time, the French continued to maintain the pressure of their attacks, some from Telnitz, others east from Augezd and still others from Sokolnitz. Some Allied troops made their escape across the Mönitz pond, whose ice also broke under their weight, but most skirted around it, toward the village of Mönitz and on southward. Many hundreds, wearied by the retreat, were rounded up by pursuing French light cavalry. The decisive defeat of the Allies was complete.

AFTER THE BATTLE

Cost and Consequences

The total of Russian losses vary, with reliable modern estimates claiming between 21,000 and 25,000 killed, wounded and captured, and about 5,600 stragglers later re-joining the army. The estimates for Austrian dead and wounded are approximately 4,200, or about 12–14 per cent of the forces engaged – a similar proportion to French losses. Again, stragglers returning to the ranks should be taken into account, leaving estimated total Allied losses at perhaps 20,000–25,000 men, of whom, according to official French records, almost 9,800 Russians and nearly 1,700 Austrians fell captive. French casualties amounted to approximately 9,000–10,000 killed, wounded or captured. Whatever the precise figures, this represented a small proportion of those engaged, considering the extent of the success achieved.

Emperor Francis arranged a meeting with Napoleon in the early hours of 3 December and offered an interview to discuss general peace. This confirmed that Napoleon had not simply defeated Austria; he had dismantled the Third Coalition by knocking the Habsburgs altogether out of the war. The two sovereigns met again, near Austerlitz, on the 4th, with Napoleon initially hopeful of pursuing the remnants of the Allied army so as to inflict the

FORTUNE FAVOURS THE BOLD

Napoleon took extraordinary risks, such as operating at a considerable distance from home soil in the depths of winter. Notwithstanding the magnitude of success achieved at Ulm, more hesitant commanders would have advanced with caution, not seeking to engage the Russians while ignorant of their strength. Not so Napoleon, who ordered a vigorous pursuit of Kutuzov east, even as substantial threats remained on the flanks of the Grande Armée and Prussia's role in the campaign remained an open question. Even when the probability of intervention increased after Bernadotte crossed into Ansbach in violation of Prussian territorial integrity, Napoleon recognised Kutuzov as the only immediate threat and remained fixed on engaging him at the earliest opportunity – before the Allies could bring substantial reinforcements to bear to compensate for the catastrophic losses sustained in Bavaria.

greatest possible damage on the Russians before an armistice could take effect. In fact, although sufficient French troops stood ready for pursuit, they had largely lost contact with Russian forces, which had begun their withdrawal towards Hungary. In the event, despite a limited French effort at pursuit on the 3rd, the Russians had made good their escape. Thus, with the Austrians left to fend for themselves, Napoleon and Francis agreed terms of an armistice to which the tsar pledged to adhere.

Having arranged for the cessation of hostilities, Napoleon returned to Vienna and briefly met the Prussian ambassador, Count Haugwitz, on 7 December. Haugwitz had always advocated peace and believed that the radically changed circumstances justified his withholding the king's Potsdam ultimatum, meant to be delivered to the French emperor, outlining the threat of Prussian intervention in the campaign. Instead, in a humiliating turn of events, Haugwitz congratulated Napoleon on his success and awaited the consequences of the campaign for his still powerful, yet now isolated, country. The emperor thereafter spent the next several weeks with Talleyrand working out the details of the peace treaty to be presented to Austria, and also considered his policy towards Prussia. He intended to deal harshly with the former and to penalise the latter for her failure to remain genuinely neutral during the campaign.

Concluded on 26 December 1805, the terms of the Treaty of Pressburg, signed in what is now Bratislava, were nothing if not harsh, starting with a war indemnity of 40 million gold francs (c. £2 million in 1805) imposed on the Habsburgs, together with demands for large territorial cessions in Italy and Germany. In the former, Pressburg reaffirmed the extensive French territorial gains achieved there as a result of the Treaty of Campo Formio in 1797 – notably Venetia, Dalmatia and Istria, territories whose cession the settlement at Lunéville confirmed in 1801 – and obliged Austria to recognise Napoleon's more recent inroads in Italy, including the annexation of Genoa and his adoption of the title of King of Italy.

Discussing peace at Schönbrunn Palace, near Vienna, where French and Austrian officials hammered out some of the terms which broke up the Third Coalition. Most of the talks took place at Pressburg (now Bratislava), which lent its name to the treaty.

The treaty also stipulated that Venetia became formally annexed to the French Empire.

In Germany, Austria was forced to cede its scattered holdings to Napoleon's three recently acquired south German allies: Bavaria, Württemberg and Baden. The first of these, for her loyalty during the campaign, acquired various territories to add to the already substantial Wittlesbach domains: the Margravate of Burgau, the Principality of Eichstadt, the Tyrol, Vorarlburg, Hohenems, Königsegg-Rothenfels, Tettnang, Argen and the city of Lindau. In Swabia, Württemberg annexed the cities of Ehingen, Munderkingen, Riedlingen, Mengen and Sulgen, as well as the county of Hohenberg, the Landgravate of Nellenbourg and the Prefecture of Altorf. Napoleon also altered the status of Bavaria from an electorate to a kingdom. Similarly, the emperor elevated the Electorate of Baden to a grand duchy, and secured for it various territories in Swabia: part of the Brisgau, the Ortenau, the city of Constance and the commandery of Meinau. By way of minor compensation, France permitted Austria to annex the Archbishopric of Salzburg (removing from power the former Grand Duke of Tuscany who had received Salzburg in 1803, but who now received Würzburg in compensation from Bavaria), Berchtesgaden and the estates of the Teutonic Order. By these means, the states of southern Germany for the first time enjoyed the benefit of contiguous territories. These major territorial losses in Germany represented the beginning of the process to conclude the following year with the formation of the Confederation of the Rhine, a body Napoleon established as a substitute for the now fatally weakened Holy Roman Empire and of which more will be said later. All told, the Habsburg Empire lost 2.5 million subjects.

The loss of Austria from the coalition influenced the conduct of the flanking attacks to be conducted by Allied forces in Hanover and the joint Anglo-Russian expedition to the Kingdom of Naples. Swedish and Russian troops reached Swedish Pomerania in early October and proceeded towards Hanover, there to be joined in the middle of the month by a British expedition landed by the Royal Navy. News of Austerlitz and later of Pressburg, however, dampened the vigour of commanders, who withdrew their forces, with British troops embarking in February 1806. The Anglo-Russian force intended for operations in southern Italy, meanwhile, arrived late, in early January 1806, and re-embarked a few days later on learning news of Austerlitz, leaving Naples to its fate. The decision of Naples to join the Third Coalition was to cost King Ferdinand IV his mainland possessions, for when the French invaded, the Bourbons could not effectively oppose them, and fled to Sicily under British protection. The authorities left behind concluded an armistice with the French on 4 February 1806 and, on 30 March, Napoleon decreed his brother, Joseph Bonaparte, King of Naples. There, as in Belgium, Holland, elsewhere in Italy and in much of Germany, Napoleonic rule led to the introduction of various reforms modelled on their

THE CORNERSTONE OF NAPOLEON'S STRATEGY

The key to the emperor's strategy lay in defeating the Allies before they could concentrate their forces against him. Thus, once he defeated Mack he aggressively pursued Kutuzov, hoping to vanquish him before he received reinforcements. This strategy also depended on Napoleon keeping the various Austrian armies in other theatres away from the Danube Valley – specifically Archdukes Charles and John in Italy and the Tyrol, respectively. As late as a decade on, during the Waterloo campaign of 1815, Napoleon would seek to defeat numerically superior opponents by engaging them separately, before they could combine forces and consolidate their strength. The emperor achieved this temporarily when he fought the Anglo-Allies at Quatre Bras and the Prussians at Ligny on 16 June, but failed to stop the bulk of the Prussians two days later from leaving Wavre and aiding Wellington's defence at Waterloo.

French counterparts, including a centralised administration, new civil and penal codes and the expropriation of Church properties. Occupation, in short, left the entire Italian peninsula under either the direct or indirect control of France.

By insisting upon the signature of a treaty of alliance, Napoleon made the most of his defeat of Austria and Russia by isolating Prussia diplomatically from its more powerful neighbours. First, the emperor obliged the king to dismiss Count Hardenberg, the chief minister, whose anti-French sentiments contributed to the king eventually signing the Treaty of Potsdam a month before Austerlitz. To entice Prussia into friendship – or at the very least, neutrality – Napoleon offered her Hanover, whose transfer was correctly calculated to alienate Prussia and Britain, with France in return receiving the principalities of Ansbach and Neuchatel, both minor territories not contiguous with Prussia herself but useful as rewards for Bavaria in the case of the former, and as a personal reward to Marshal Berthier in the case of the latter.

Napoleon and Haugwitz met on 14 December 1805, when the former presented his terms. Haugwitz felt he had no room for negotiation, given Austria's defeat and the absence from Moravia of the Russian Army. The French now stood in a position to confront Prussia at will and were already marching to oppose the small expeditionary forces landed in Hanover and Naples. Nearly 200,000 Prussians were theoretically available to fight the French, but in light of the decisive defeat inflicted on Austria and the humiliating retreat of the Russians, Haugwitz felt the gamble too great to risk. Thus, on 15 December, he signed the Treaty of Schonbrünn and sent it to Berlin for the king's ratification. There, officials sought to modify its terms, but Napoleon dismissed them; two months later, with massive French forces arrayed across southern Germany and war a real possibility, Frederick William accepted the terms, transferring Hanover to Prussia, but forbidden the right to open his new acquisition to British shipping, thus denying Prussia much of the wealth in trade she had hoped to secure by virtue of annexation.

Prussia's policy of neutrality during the campaign had failed in both its objectives: either to avoid confrontation with France by remaining inactive or to intervene in a manner which turned the tide against France and thereby guaranteed Prussia a dominant role in the distribution of the spoils of war at the peace conference to follow. In the event, Frederick William's vacillation had weakened him considerably, for by failing to participate in the campaign he inadvertently strengthened French power in Germany; later antagonised Britain by his annexation of Hanover and his adherence to French economic policy; inherited a possession which though ostensibly beneficial to her, actually harmed Prussia's economy given the trade restrictions imposed by Napoleon; and in general left Prussia subservient to France. It was precisely this position which would, in the autumn of 1806, drive Prussia into war – but without allies immediately to hand. Britain could offer nothing more than subsidies and Russian forces were too far east to intervene in the opening campaign in Saxony.

Austria's substantial reductions of power in Italy and, above all, Germany did not end with the terms of the Treaty of Pressburg, for seven months later Austria lost her centuries-old dominance in Germany as a result of the creation of the Confederation of the Rhine (Rheinbund): a conglomeration of German states organised by Napoleon who hoped that Germany would develop into a unified state with a central government and administration, modelling the political institutions of France. First, the Imperial Reichstag (the parliament of the thousand-year-old Holy Roman Empire) was abolished on 20 January 1806, enabling Napoleon to create the first of a new set of minor German states to be ruled by members of his family. On 15 March, for instance, he established the Grand Duchy of Berg, placing his brother-in-law, Murat, at its head. Then the Confederation of the Rhine came into formal being on 17 July 1806, according to the Treaty of Paris, with Karl Theodor von Dalberg as prince-primate (*Fürstenprimas*) and Napoleon maintaining supervisory control in his capacity as protector (*Protektor*) – in effect, establishing a body of states within the French sphere of influence and hosting a permanent French garrison. The original sixteen south and west German states of the Confederation consisted of Bavaria, Württemberg, Hesse-Darmstadt, Baden, Berg and eleven other smaller states, all of which, according to the Rheinbund's constitution, formally withdrew from the Holy Roman Empire, which drew its last breath on 6 August when Francis II foreswore the Habsburgs' ancient imperial dignity and proclaimed himself Francis I, Emperor of Austria, in its place.

As an inducement to membership in the new Confederation – which, however, was effectively coerced – Napoleon offered an extension of territory and elevation in rank. Thus, as we have seen, he raised the electors of Bavaria (Maximilian Joseph) and of the Grand Duchy of Württemberg (Frederick II) to the status of kings on 1 January 1806, made the electors of Baden and Hesse-Darmstadt grand dukes on 13 August and offered similar titles

Napoleon declares the formation of the Confederation of the Rhine, a body of German states owing direct or indirect allegiance to the emperor – just one of many of the important consequences of French victory in the 1805 campaign.

to other minor potentates. The Grand Duchy of Würzburg joined on 23 September. Saxony, Prussia's only immediately available ally during the Jena-Auerstädt campaign fought the following month, would join the Confederation in the wake of her defeat.

Thus, the destruction of the Third Coalition enabled Napoleon to dismantle the Holy Roman Empire and replace it with an entirely new, subservient German political entity, which could serve as a territorial buffer against Prussia and Austria, offer a sizeable, proximate market for French goods and provide a source of military manpower for the growing Napoleonic empire. In short, by stripping Austria of the remainder of her power and influence in Central Europe, Napoleon found himself in a position to recast German affairs.

By shattering the cohesion of the Third Coalition, Austerlitz put an end to the Allies' efforts to stem the expansion of France, which had begun in 1792. Pressburg marked out precisely the magnitude of Austria's share in the defeat, for it ended the Habsburgs' dominant role in Central Europe – a process begun by the Prussian king Frederick II ('the Great') in the two wars against Maria Theresa over Silesia in the mid-eighteenth century and accelerated by the French Revolutionary Wars in its closing years. Tens of thousands of prisoners lay in French hands owing to the series of capitulations in October, the remainder of the army reeled from the shock of being vanquished in battle and the loss of what remained of her influence in Germany and Italy left the Habsburg Empire a shadow of its former self.

Apart from Waterloo, Austerlitz stands unchallenged for the political implications which resulted from its outcome, for in enabling Napoleon to lay the foundations of an empire which extended well into Central Europe, it encouraged his further expansion and consolidation until, as a consequence of the remarkable campaigns of 1806–07, France held a seemingly unassailable position of power on the Continent.

THE LEGACY

A Further Decade of Conflict:

Trying to Force the Napoleonic Genie back into its Bottle
The War of the Fourth Coalition (1806–07)

Despite the collapse of the Third Coalition, Europe did not return to peace; on the contrary, it was to be convulsed by war for the next decade, until the final denouement at Waterloo in June 1815. It is instructive, therefore, to view Austerlitz in the context of the remainder of the Napoleonic Wars, examining how, despite the decisive nature of that battle, France eventually fell victim to a fatal case of what may today be called 'imperial overstretch'.

Although Austria withdrew from the coalition after Austerlitz, Britain and Russia remained at war with France. Prussia, having foolishly failed to commit herself to the contest in 1805, when she could have played an instrumental role in its outcome had she joined with Austria and Russia, threw in her lot, unilaterally, in the autumn of 1805. The Fourth Coalition came into being after a breakdown in Franco-Prussian relations, which was largely the result of Napoleon's failure to cede Hanover to Prussia, as promised – in fact, in abortive peace proposals to Britain in the summer of 1806, he offered to restore Hanover to George III – and owing to the establishment of the Confederation of the Rhine. Concerned at the growing influence of France in German affairs, Prussia, together with its ally, the Electorate of Saxony, declared war – but prematurely, for the Russians could not intervene rapidly enough to have a bearing on the opening campaign.

The Grande Armée, situated in north-east Bavaria, prepared to invade Prussia, whose forces fell under the command of the Duke of Brunswick, a veteran of the wars of Frederick the Great. With remarkable speed, the French began their advance on 8 October, achieving complete surprise. Marshal Lannes, in a minor action at Saalfeld on 10 October, defeated a small Prussian force and killed Prince Louis Ferdinand of Prussia, while the main French Army turned the Prussian left flank as it made for Berlin. Napoleon fought part of the main Prussian Army under Count Hohenlohe at Jena on 14 October. Hohenlohe's command was, however, merely a small force meant to protect Brunswick's rear; Napoleon's numerical superiority predictably told, and Hohenlohe was

The Battle of Jena, 14 October 1806. Fought simultaneously with a much larger engagement at Auerstädt, Jena holds a special place in the pantheon of great Napoleonic victories – nearly on a par with Austerlitz.

routed. At Auerstädt, a short distance to the north, on the same day, Davout, who had been sent to cut Prussian communications, encountered the main Prussian force under Brunswick. There the odds were rather different, with Davout outnumbered by a force more than twice the size of his own. He managed to hold on, however, and when Bernadotte arrived, the tide turned decisively in the French favour, with the Prussians routed there as well, and the Duke of Brunswick mortally wounded.

The destruction of Prussia's main army effectively spelled the end of resistance, and the remainder of the campaign consisted of the French pursuit of small contingents, virtually all of which eventually put down their arms, and the capture of fortresses. Berlin itself fell on 24 October, and the last major force to hold out, near Lübeck, surrendered a month later. A small Prussian contingent managed to make contact with the Russians in Poland, while the French occupied Warsaw in an effort to prevent the Russians from assisting their vanquished allies.

Adhering to the principle that the key to victory lay in confronting and decisively defeating the main enemy force, Napoleon sought out the Russian Army under General Bennigsen, the first encounter taking place on 26 December at Pultusk, where the Russians were bruised but nothing more. The rival armies went into winter quarters in January 1807 amid bitterly cold temperatures, but the campaign resumed the following month, when Bennigsen began to move and Napoleon went in pursuit. Though outnumbered and caught in a blizzard, Napoleon reached the Russians at Eylau, where on 8 February the two sides inflicted severe losses on one another with no decisive result. Bennigsen withdrew, but with appalling losses and atrocious weather, Napoleon declined to follow. Both sides returned to winter quarters to recover from the carnage, with the renewal of hostilities planned for the spring.

Bennigsen and Napoleon each planned to assume the offensive, but when Bennigsen advanced first, he was stopped at Heilsberg on 10 June. Four days later the decisive encounter of the campaign

Napoleon surveys the battlefield at Friedland, where on 14 June 1807 he decisively defeated the Russians, putting paid to the Fourth Coalition.

took place at Friedland, where Bennigsen foolishly placed his army with the River Alle at his back. The Russians resisted enemy attacks with magnificent stoicism, but eventually collapsed. With no route of escape, the campaign was over. Tsar Alexander, his army in tatters, and accompanied at headquarters by Frederick William III of Prussia, requested a conference to discuss peace. The three sovereigns concluded the Treaty of Tilsit between 7 and 9 July, putting the seal on Napoleonic control of Western Europe. Frederick William was humiliated, forfeiting those portions of his Polish possessions originally taken during the partitions of Poland more than a decade before to the newly established Duchy of Warsaw, a French satellite state. To the Confederation of the Rhine, Prussia ceded all its territory between the Rhine and the Elbe, most of this forming the new Kingdom of Westphalia under Napoleon's brother, Jerome. A French army of occupation was to remain on Prussian soil until a huge war indemnity was paid. Russia was required to enter into an alliance with France against Britain and to recognise the Duchy of Warsaw. With Russia and

Prussia knocked out of the war, only Britain remained to face France, now at the height of its power.

The War of the Fifth Coalition (1809)

In the aftermath of the Austerlitz campaign, Archduke Charles instituted wide-scale reforms across the army, though when war loomed in 1809 he did not feel Austria was ready to fight. The Fifth Coalition hardly justified the name, for when Austria once again chose to oppose France, it did so without allies to assist it on land. Britain, of course, carried on operations at sea and offered substantial subsidies and loans, as it had since 1793, but it could do little more on land than send an expedition in July 1809 to Walcheren Island, off the Dutch coast, where disease soon rendered the whole affair a disaster and obliged the British to withdraw in October. Nevertheless, the Austrians had some reason to be hopeful, for in fielding a sizeable army in the spring of 1809, they took advantage of the absence from Central Europe of large numbers of French troops, which had been diverted to serve in operations in Spain. Yet, with misplaced optimism, they underestimated Napoleon's ability to muster his forces and concentrate them quickly, for by the time the Habsburg armies were ready to fight, the French had shifted reinforcements from the Iberian Peninsula to meet this revived threat.

The main Austrian Army, under Archduke Charles, invaded the principal member of the Confederation of the Rhine, Bavaria, which also had to contend with an Austrian-inspired revolt in the Tyrol, a region formerly under Habsburg control. At the same time, Archduke John crossed the Alps to invade northern Italy, repulsing Eugène at Sacile on 16 April. When Napoleon arrived from Spain, he moved immediately to the offensive, crossing the Danube and defeating an Austrian force at Abensberg on 19–20 April before turning on Charles, then under observation by Davout. Charles struck first, confronting Davout at Eggmühl but failing, despite overwhelming numerical superiority, to defeat him, as a result of Napoleon's arrival. French exhaustion from three days' engagements (at Abensberg, Landshut and Eggmühl) denied them the opportunity to pursue Charles, though they managed to storm and seize Ratisbon on 23 April. Three weeks later French troops occupied Vienna without a shot being fired.

Charles, meanwhile, concentrated his army on the north bank of the Danube. Napoleon ordered pontoon bridges constructed to span the river to Lobau Island, and then to the other side, where troops positioned themselves in the villages of Aspern and Essling. On 21–22 May, the two sides fought bitterly for possession of these villages, but the French refused to be dislodged. However, with the single French bridge unable to allow substantial numbers of reinforcements to be fed to the north side of the river, Napoleon withdrew his forces to the opposite bank, marking out Aspern-Essling as the emperor's first defeat. Napoleon intended to re-cross the Danube and confront Charles for a second time, but he knew he must first develop another plan to do so. Meanwhile, on the Italian front, Archduke John was obliged to withdraw back over the Julian Alps, followed up by Eugène, who was successful at Raab on 16 June and subsequently moved to link up with the main French Army on the Danube.

Hoping to defeat Charles before he could be reinforced by Archduke John, Napoleon re-crossed the Danube on the night of 4/5 July. The Austrians offered no resistance to the crossing, but on the 5th and 6th heavy fighting took place at Wagram, where Charles attempted to isolate Napoleon from his bridgehead. This manoeuvre, however, failed; the Austrian centre was pierced and Charles was obliged to retreat, albeit with very heavy losses suffered by both sides. Austria could no longer carry on the war. Vienna was under enemy occupation, the main army had been beaten, though not destroyed, and Russia had not joined the campaign as Austria had hoped. Francis duly sued for peace on 10 July and three months later signed the Treaty of Schönbrunn, by which he relinquished large portions of his empire to France and its allies and promised to adhere to Napoleon's Continental

System, by which the emperor sought to impose an embargo on the importation of British goods to the Continent and the exportation of continental goods to Britain in an effort to strangle the latter's economy.

The Peninsular War (1807–14)

Quite separate from the other campaigns waged in Europe, the Peninsular War, fought on the Iberian Peninsula, constituted the principal theatre in which Britain could at last contribute substantial land forces to the war against Napoleon. Portuguese and, above all, Spanish resistance, involving both regular and guerrilla forces, over time contributed much to the diversion of French troops from other theatres of conflict, and to the continual drain on French manpower. After the Treaty of Tilsit and the introduction of the Continental System, only Portugal continued to defy the ban by accepting British imports. In an effort to close this final avenue of trade, Napoleon sent troops through Spain to Portugal, taking advantage of the opportunity to impose his will on the Spanish as well.

In November 1807, General Junot began his march through Spain, entering Lisbon in December. The Portuguese royal family was evacuated by the Royal Navy and transported to Brazil, while the provisional government left behind sought assistance from Britain. Napoleon then revealed his full intentions when in March 1808 Marshal Murat entered Spain at the head of a large army, occupied Spanish fortresses and disarmed their garrisons under false pretences, and deposed both King Charles IV and his son Ferdinand, who were replaced by Napoleon's brother Joseph, backed by pro-Bonapartist elements in Madrid. The French occupation was never fated to go smoothly; on 2 May, the populace of Madrid rose up in revolt, and the spirit of resistance soon spread throughout the country, where guerrilla bands began to spring up and prey on French detachments, couriers and isolated outposts. The regular Spanish armies fought a number of pitched battles against the French in 1808–09, but they were generally defeated, sometimes disastrously. Spanish resistance also manifested itself in a number of epic sieges in which civilians played a prominent part, most notably that of Saragossa, north-east of Madrid, where in the summer of 1808 the inhabitants managed to stave off repeated French attempts to storm the city. The one significant Spanish success in the field came at Bailén, in Andalusia, where on 19 July 1808, General Dupont surrendered an army of 23,000 men, sending shock waves across Europe and destroying the myth of French invincibility.

The war in the peninsula took on an entirely different character from August 1808, when a British expeditionary force led by Lieutenant General Sir Arthur Wellesley (later the Duke of Wellington) arrived in Portugal and defeated Junot at Vimeiro on 21 August, thus securing a foothold for the British Army. By the Convention of Cintra, senior British commanders granted the French generous terms, which allowed them to be transported home with their weapons and loot in British ships. Wellesley alone was cleared by the court of inquiry that convened in London and cashiered the generals responsible for what in Britain were considered the disgraceful terms agreed to at Cintra.

With Portugal cleared of French troops and British reinforcements arriving under Lieutenant General Sir John Moore, an opportunity now offered itself for an offensive into Spain. Moore, with promises of Spanish support, therefore advanced in the autumn of 1808. When Spanish troops failed to materialise, however, Moore faced numerically superior forces under Napoleon himself, who had arrived in Spain determined to drive the British out of the Iberian Peninsula once and for all. He occupied Madrid on 4 December and pursued the British commander, obliging Moore to make a long, punishing retreat amidst winter conditions to Corunna (and another, smaller column to retreat to Vigo) on the north-west Spanish coast. The diversion of French attention toward the retreating British columns gave the Spanish armies a much-needed respite. Believing Moore to be at risk of imminent retreat at the hands of Marshal Soult, and with war looming with Austria, Napoleon left for France. Moore was harassed for much of the journey, but on reaching Corunna he turned to face Soult before evacuating his troops on to Royal Navy transports. Moore died in the ensuing battle, but his ragged army was saved, and by that time Lisbon had been sufficiently fortified to prevent the French from retaking it. Saragossa, however, finally surrendered, after a second enormously costly siege in February 1809.

Wellesley returned to Portugal in command of the army there, to be supplemented by Portuguese forces reorganised on the British model by Marshal Beresford. Soult invaded Portugal in the spring of 1809, but Wellesley ejected him after fighting at Oporto, on the Douro River, on 12 May. Exploiting his success, Wellesley crossed the border into Spain to co-operate with the Spanish commander, General García de la Cuesta, who in the event failed to assist Wellesley at Talavera on 28 July, when he came under attack by Marshal Victor and Joseph Bonaparte. The Anglo-Portuguese forces narrowly held off the French, for which Wellesley was rewarded with elevation to the peerage as Marquis Wellington, finishing the Peninsular War as the Duke of Wellington. Meanwhile, the Spanish armies showed themselves to be incapable of confronting the French, who defeated them comprehensively at Ocaña on 19 November. Unable to take the war into Spain, for the moment Wellington concentrated on defending Portugal, where Lisbon was established as an easily accessible base where supplies and troops could be landed from Britain, and which held complete command of the maritime route from home. Wellington ensured that the defences could sustain an attack on any scale by ordering the construction of a line of impregnable fortifications, known later as the Lines of Torres Vedras, across the peninsula on which Lisbon is situated.

Massena opened the campaign of 1810 with yet another French invasion of Portugal, in July, but he was defeated at Busaco on 27 September by Wellington, who then withdrew behind the protection afforded by the completed lines of Torres

Vedras. Massena followed him, but upon discovering the lines he made one attempt at penetrating them before realising that they were unassailable. He therefore camped his troops before the lines for the remainder of the year and into 1811, with very little food to be foraged or requisitioned in the area, as a result of Wellington's scorched earth policy. The French also sought to capture Cádiz, in the far south of the country, where the Spanish had established an alternative capital to occupied Madrid. At Cádiz a small British force under Sir Thomas Graham repulsed the French at Barrosa on 5 March, securing the port city's safety. Massena fought Wellington at Fuentes de Oñoro on 5–7 May, while to the south Beresford's Anglo-Spanish army beat Soult, himself seeking to aid French troops besieged at Badajoz. Losses were very heavy on both sides, and though Soult was unable to relieve the garrison, the fortress remained in French hands and thus prevented Wellington from taking the war into Spain. The French were successful elsewhere: in the south, Marshal Louis Suchet captured Tarragona on 28 July 1811 and Valencia on 9 January 1812.

The campaign of 1812 opened with Wellington assuming the offensive, seizing the border fortresses of Ciudad Rodrigo on 19 January and Badajoz on 6 April, the latter taken only after the British storming parties suffered tremendous losses in a series of desperate assaults. Notwithstanding the heavy price paid for possession of these towns, Wellington could at last carry the war into Spain, where he scored a decisive victory over Marshal Marmont at Salamanca on 22 July. Wellington occupied Madrid for a short time in August, but with the failure of his assault on Burgos as a result of inadequate siege equipment, he was obliged to retreat as far as Portugal. Nevertheless, large numbers of French troops had been withdrawn for the Russian campaign, and years of guerrilla operations had inflicted a heavy toll on both French strength and morale.

In 1813 Wellington was enabled to return to the offensive, routing Joseph's army at Vitoria on 21 June, thus ending

Bonapartist rule and forcing the French from most of the country to a narrow band of territory in the extreme north. Wellington continued to drive the French before him, taking San Sebastian and Pamplona, and fighting his way through several passes in the Pyrenees to invade France itself. He defeated Soult, first at Orthez on 27 February 1814 and again in the final major action of the war on 10 April at Toulouse, where news had not yet arrived that Napoleon had already abdicated in Paris a few days earlier.

The Peninsular War had not only brought to the fore one of Britain's greatest commanders, it had drained French resources over the course of many years, thus making an important contribution to Napoleon's ultimate downfall.

The Russian Campaign (1812)

With the Continental System eventually cutting hard into the Russian economy and Alexander growing increasingly concerned about the presence of the Duchy of Warsaw on his borders, war between Russia and France became inevitable. Napoleon, gathering a massive army of unprecedented size and composed of every nationality from his empire, pushed across the Niemen River with over half a million men on 22 June 1812. The two main Russian armies, one under General Barclay de Tolly and the other under Bagration, found themselves unable to resist a force of this size, and withdrew east, uniting at Smolensk on 3 August. Unable to outflank his opponents, Napoleon chose to engage them first on 17 August at Smolensk, where he took the city by storm, and again at Valutino two days later, where he scored a minor success, the Russians simply withdrawing deeper into the interior and obliging the French to extend their increasingly vulnerable lines of communication even further.

The Russian commander-in-chief, Barclay de Tolly, was replaced by Kutuzov, who on 7 September made an extremely hard-fought stand at Borodino, where rather than attempting any elaborate manoeuvres to envelop the stationary Russians, Napoleon launched a simple frontal assault against prepared positions held by troops committed to defend 'Holy Russia' with the utmost determination. The battle degenerated into a horrendous blood-letting with no decisive result. Kutuzov withdrew further east, with the exhausted French unable to pursue in the short term. The Russians made no further attempt to defend Moscow, which the French entered on 14 September. Nevertheless, much of the city was almost immediately destroyed by fire – probably deliberately set by the Russians – though enough remained of Moscow to provide shelter for Napoleon's dwindling army for the month that the emperor chose to remain there, all the while hoping that the tsar would sue for peace. Alexander sent no such overtures, and by the time Napoleon began his retreat on 19 October, winter had nearly arrived.

The story of the retreat from Moscow is well known: snow soon began to fall, and the army, harassed by Cossacks and suffering from hunger, cold and lack of horse-drawn transport, disintegrated into a mass of fugitives, most of whom could offer little or no resistance to the increasingly vengeful Russians. The entire path of the army became strewn with bodies, abandoned

The remnants of the once-formidable Grande Armée fleeing across the Berezina River during the retreat from Moscow in the winter of 1812.

equipment and the spoils of war. On 24 October, the Russians caught up with the corps, mostly Italians, under Eugène at Maloyaroslavets, inflicting a serious blow, and when the army finally reached Smolensk it was hardly worthy of the name. Stragglers and camp followers were regularly butchered by the Cossacks, and discipline and morale gradually collapsed. Kutuzov cut off part of the Grande Armée at Krasnyi on 16–17 November, though Napoleon managed to rescue it, and the whole struggled on to the Berezina River. There, engineers, working under the most difficult circumstances, managed to throw two makeshift bridges across the river, enabling thousands to cross, while what units could be cobbled together fought on the east bank to hold back the attacks of the regular Russian Army. Eventually the bridges gave way under the weight of the fugitives, leaving thousands to be captured or killed on the Russian side of the river. Fewer than 100,000 survivors eventually reached the Niemen at the end of December, when the Russians halted their pursuit of an army that had dissolved into mere rabble. The Grande Armée had effectively ceased to exist, but Napoleon had already gone ahead to Paris to assemble a new army.

The Campaign in Germany (1813)

However immense the losses suffered by Napoleon in Russia, his extraordinary administrative skills enabled him to rebuild his army by the spring of 1813, though neither the men nor the horses could be replaced in their former quality or quantity. The Sixth Coalition, which had been formed by Britain, Russia, Spain and Portugal in June 1812, now expanded as other states became emboldened to oppose Napoleonic hegemony in Europe. The Prussian corps, which had reluctantly accompanied the Grande Armée into Russia, declared its neutrality by the Convention of Tauroggen on 30 December 1812, and on 27 February 1813 Frederick William formally brought his country into the coalition by the terms of the Convention of Kalisch, signed with Russia.

The Austrians remained neutral during the spring campaign, with General Schwarzenberg's corps, which had covered the southern flank of the French advance into Russia, withdrawing into Bohemia.

By the time the campaign began in the spring, Napoleon had created new fighting formations from the ashes of the old, calling up men who had been exempted from military service in the past, those who had been previously discharged but could be classed as generally fit and those who, owing to their youth, would not normally have been eligible for front-line duty for at least another year. With such poorly trained and inexperienced, yet still enthusiastic, troops, Napoleon occupied the Saxon capital, Dresden, on 7–8 May, and defeated General Wittgenstein, first at Lützen on 2 May and again at Bautzen on 20–21 May. Both sides agreed to an armistice, which stretched from June through July and into mid-August, during which time the French recruited and trained their green army, while the Allies assembled larger and larger forces, now to include Austrians, Swedes and troops from a number of former members of the Confederation of the Rhine.

When the campaign resumed, the Allies deployed three multinational armies in the field: one under Schwarzenberg, one under Blücher and a third under Napoleon's former marshal, Bernadotte. The Allies formulated a new strategy, known as the Trachenberg Plan, by which they would seek to avoid direct confrontation with the main French Army under Napoleon, instead concentrating their efforts against the emperor's subordinates, whom they would seek to defeat in turn. The plan succeeded: Bernadotte drubbed Oudinot at Grossbeeren on 23 August, and Blücher won against Macdonald at the Katzbach River three days later. Napoleon, for his part, scored a significant victory against Schwarzenberg at Dresden on 26–27 August, but the emperor failed to pursue the Austrian commander. Shortly thereafter, Vandamme's corps became isolated during its pursuit of Schwarzenberg and was annihilated at Kulm on 29–30 August.

The end of French control of Germany was nearing. First, Bernadotte defeated Ney at Dennewitz on 6 September; then Bavaria, the principal member of the Confederation of the Rhine, defected to the Allies. The decisive battle of the campaign was fought at Leipzig from 16–19 October, when all three main Allied armies converged on the city to attack Napoleon's positions in and around it. In the largest battle in history up to that time, both sides suffered extremely heavy losses, and though part of the Grande Armée crossed the River Elster and escaped before the bridge was blown, the Allies nevertheless achieved a victory of immense proportions, which forced the French out of Germany and back across the Rhine. A Bavarian force under Wrede tried to stop Napoleon's retreat at Hanau on 30–31 October, but the French managed to push through to reach home soil a week later. Napoleon, his allies having either deserted his cause or found themselves under Allied occupation, now prepared to oppose the invasion of France by numerically superior armies converging on several fronts.

The Campaign in France (1814)

Convinced that he could still recover his vast territorial losses, Napoleon chose to fight on against all the odds, rejecting offers from the Allies that would have left France with its 'natural' frontiers: the Rhine, the Alps and the Pyrenees. French forces were under pressure on several fronts: Wellington's Anglo-Portuguese and Spanish forces stood poised along the French side of the Pyrenees; the Austrians were already operating in northern Italy; and several armies were making seemingly inexorable progress from the east – Schwarzenberg approaching from Switzerland, Blücher through eastern France and Bernadotte from the north through the Netherlands. To oppose these impressive forces, Napoleon possessed little more than a small army consisting of hastily raised units, National Guardsmen and anyone who had somehow avoided the call-ups of the past. Somehow, at least in the initial stages of the campaign, the emperor managed to summon up the kind of energy and tactical brilliance for which he had become renowned during the Italian campaigns of 1796–97.

In swift succession, he drubbed Blücher at Brienne on 29 January 1814, at La Rothière on 30 January, at Champaubert on 10 February, at Montmirail on 11 February, at Château-Thierry on 12 February and at Vauchamps on 14 February. Napoleon then turned to confront Schwarzenberg at Montereau on 18 February, before again fighting Blücher at Craonne, near Paris, on 7 March. Yet, however many enemies he could repel in turn, Napoleon could not be everywhere at once, and his corps commanders, despite the continued enthusiasm for battle displayed by the troops themselves, could not achieve the same results in the field as the emperor. The French could not stand up to the numbers facing them at Laon on 9–10 March, and though there were still successes in March, such as at Arcis-sur-Aube on 20–21 March, Schwarzenberg then defeated two of Napoleon's subordinates at La-Fère-Champenoise on 25 March, before linking up with Blücher on the 28th.

The Allies were now very close to Paris, where Joseph Bonaparte had failed to make adequate provision for the capital's defence. After token resistance at Clichy and Montmartre on 30 March, Marmont refused to fight on, and the Allies entered the capital the following day. At a conference with his marshals, Napoleon found himself surrounded by men finally prepared to defy him; the troops, they declared, would listen to their generals, not the emperor. With no alternative, Napoleon abdicated unconditionally on 11 April and, by the terms of the Treaty of Paris, took up residence on Elba, off the Italian coast, while the Bourbon line in France was restored under King Louis XVIII.

The Waterloo Campaign (1815)

Napoleon was not content to remain on Elba and manage the affairs of his tiny island kingdom. Landing in France in March 1815 with a small band of followers, he marched on Paris, gathering loyal veterans and adherents from the army as he went, including Ney, whom the king had specifically sent to apprehend the pretender to the throne. Allied leaders were at the time assembled at Vienna, there to redraw the map of Europe, which had been so radically revised by more than two decades of war. The Seventh Coalition was soon on the march, with effectively the whole of Europe in arms and marching to defeat Napoleon before he could raise sufficient troops to hold off the overwhelming numbers that the Allies had now set in motion towards the French frontiers. With speed characteristic of his earlier days in uniform, Napoleon quickly moved north to confront the only Allied forces within reach: an Anglo-Dutch army under Wellington and a Prussian one under Blücher, both in Belgium. Napoleon could only hope to survive against the massive onslaught that would soon reach France by defeating the Allied armies separately; to this end he sought to keep Wellington and Blücher – who together easily outnumbered him – apart.

On 16 June, after a rapid march that caught Wellington, then at Brussels, entirely off guard, Napoleon detached Ney to seize the crossroads at Quatre Bras, then occupied by part of Wellington's army, while, with the main body of the Armée du Nord, the emperor moved to strike Blücher at Ligny. Ney failed in his objective, and though on the same day Napoleon delivered a sharp blow against the Prussians, the crucial result was that the two Allied armies continued to remain within supporting distance of one another. Blücher, having promised to support Wellington if he were attacked by Napoleon's main body, took up a position at Wavre, eleven miles east of Waterloo. Two days later, Napoleon did precisely that, attacking both Blücher's and Wellington's forces at separate, simultaneous engagements while the two Allied armies lay apart. Having, in the wake of the actions at Ligny and Quatre Bras, detached Marshal Grouchy to follow the Prussians, who had halted at Wavre, and prevent them from linking up with Wellington, the former emperor launched a frontal assault on Wellington's strong position around Mont St Jean, near Waterloo, on 18 June.

The hard-pressed Allied troops held on throughout the day, gradually reinforced by elements of Blücher's army who managed to leave Wavre while Grouchy, busily engaged with a Prussian holding force, refused to march to the sound of the guns at Waterloo. The French made strenuous efforts to dislodge Wellington's troops, who in turn showed exceptional determination to hold their ground, and as the Prussians gradually made their presence felt on the French right flank, the battle began to turn in the Allies' favour. In a final gamble to break Wellington's centre and clinch victory, Napoleon sent forward the Imperial Guard, but when his veterans recoiled from the intense, point-blank musket and artillery fire they received on the slope, the rest of the army dissolved into a full-scale rout.

With no possibility of retaining power, Napoleon abdicated in Paris a few days later. By the second Treaty of Paris, the Bourbons were restored to the throne for the second time, France was reduced to her pre-1792 borders, forced to support an army of occupation and pay a sizeable indemnity. As for Napoleon, his hopes of obtaining permission to reside in Britain were dashed; on surrendering himself, he was taken as a captive to spend the remainder of his life on the remote South Atlantic island of St Helena, where he died on 5 May 1821.

ORDERS OF BATTLE

The Grande Armée at Austerlitz

Commander-in-Chief: Emperor Napoleon
Chief of Staff: Marshal Berthier
Total strength of the army including staff: 74,500
Approximately 605 staff personnel, 58,135 infantry, 11,540 cavalry, 4,220 artillery and train and 157 guns

Imperial Guard: Marshal Bessières

Total strength approximately: 3,885 infantry, 1,130 cavalry, 660 artillery and train, 24 guns

Infantry of the Imperial Guard

Général de brigade (GB) Hulin
  Grenadiers à pied (2 btns)
Brigade: GB Soulès
  Chasseurs à pied (2 btns)
Royal Italian Guard (Col Lecchi)
  Grenadiers à pied (1 btn)
  Chasseurs à pied (1 btn)

Cavalry of the Imperial Guard

Brigade: GB Ordener
  Grenadiers à cheval (4 sqns)
Brigade: Col Morland
  Chasseurs à cheval (4 sqns)
  Mamelukes (½ sqn)

Reserve Grenadiers: GD Oudinot and GD Duroc

Total strength approximately: 4,650 infantry, 0 cavalry, 340 artillery and train, 8 guns
Brigade: GB Mortières
  1er Grenadier Regiment (2 btns)
  2ème Grenadier Regiment (2 btns)
Brigade: GB Dupas
  3ème Grenadier Regiment (2 btns)
  4ème Grenadier Regiment (2 btns)
Brigade: GB Ruffin
  5ème Grenadier Regiment (2 btns)

I Corps: Marshal Bernadotte

Total strength approximately: 10,900 infantry, 0 cavalry, 420 artillery and train, 22 guns

1er Division: GD Rivaud
Brigade: GB Dumoulin
   8ème *Ligne* (3 btns)
Brigade: GB Pacthod
   45ème *Ligne* (3 btns)
   54ème *Ligne* (3 btns)

2ème Division: GD Drouet
Brigade: GB Frere
   27ème *Légère* (3 btns)
Brigade: GB Werlé
   94ème *Ligne* (3 btns)
   95ème *Ligne* (3 btns)

III Corps: Marshal Davout

Total strength approximately: 3,200 infantry, 830 cavalry, 190 artillery and train, 12 guns

2ème Division: GD Friant
Brigade: GB Kister
   15ème *Légère* (2 btns, minus the voltigeurs)
   33ème *Ligne* (2 btns)
Brigade: GB Lochet
   48ème *Ligne* (2 btns)
   111ème *Ligne* (2 btns)
Brigade: GB Heudelet
   15ème *Légère* (2 btns)
   108ème *Ligne* (2 btns)

Attached to III Corps from the Cavalry Reserve
4ème Dragoon Division:
GB Bourcier
Brigade: GB Sahuc
   15ème Dragoons (3 sqns)
   17ème Dragoons (3 sqns)

Brigade: GB Laplanche
   18ème Dragoons (3 sqns)
   19ème Dragoons (3 sqns)
Brigade: GB Verdière
   25ème Dragoons (3 sqns)
   27ème Dragoons (3 sqns)

Attached (independently) to III Corps from 4ème Dragoon Division of the Cavalry Reserve
   1èr Dragoons (3 sqns)

IV Corps: Marshal Soult

Total strength approximately: 22,700 infantry, 2,650 cavalry, 1,320 artillery and train, 38 guns

1er Division: GD Saint Hilaire
Brigade: GB Morand
   10ème *Légère* (2 btns)
Brigade: GB Thiébault
   14ème *Ligne* (2 btns)
   36ème *Ligne* (2 btns)
Brigade: GB Varé
   43ème *Ligne* (2 btns)
   55ème *Ligne* (2 btns)

2ème Division: GD Vandamme
Brigade: GB Schiner
   24ère *Légère* (2 btns)
Brigade: GB Ferrey
   4ème *Ligne* (2 btns)
   28ème *Ligne* (2 btns)
Brigade: GB Candras
   46ème *Ligne* (2 btns)
   57ème *Ligne* (2 btns)

3ème Division: GD Legrand
Brigade: GB Merle
   26ème *Légère* (2 btns)
   Tirailleurs du Po (1 btn)
   Tirailleurs du Corse (1 btn)

Brigade: GB Féry
3ème *Ligne* (3 btns)
Brigade: GB Lavasseur
18ème *Ligne* (2 btns)
75ème *Ligne* (2 btns)

Light Cavalry Brigade

Brigade: GB Margaron
8ème Hussars (3 sqns)
11ème *Chasseurs à cheval* (4 sqns)
26ème *Chasseurs à cheval* (3 sqns)

Attached to IV Corps from the Cavalry Reserve

3ème Dragoon Division:

GD Beaumont
Brigade: GB Boyé
5ème Dragoons (3 sqns)
8ème Dragoons (3 sqns)
12ème Dragoons (3 sqns)
Brigade: GB Scalfort
9ème Dragoons
16ème Dragoons
21ème Dragoons

V Corps: Marshal Lannes

Total strength approximately: 12,800 infantry, 1,130 cavalry, 500 artillery and train, 23 guns

3ère Division: GD Suchet

Brigade: GB Claparède
17ème *Légère* (2 btns)
Brigade: GB Beker
34ème *Ligne* (3 btns)
40ème *Ligne* (2 btns)
Brigade: GB Valhubert
64ème *Ligne* (2 btns)
88ème *Ligne* (2 btns)

Attached from III Corps

1er Division: GD Caffarelli
Brigade: GB Eppler
13ème *Légère* (2 btns)
Brigade: GB Demont
17ème *Ligne* (2 btns)
30ème *Ligne* (2 btns)
Brigade: GB Debilly
51ème *Ligne* (2 btns)
61ème *Ligne* (2 btns)

Attached to V Corps from the Cavalry Reserve

2ème Dragoon Division:

GD Walther
Brigade: GB Sébastiani
3ème Dragoons (3 sqns)
6ème Dragoons (3 sqns)
Brigade: GB Roget
10ème Dragoons (3 sqns)
11ème Dragoons (3 sqns)
Brigade: GB Boussart
13ème Dragoons (3 sqns)
22ème Dragoons (3 sqns)

Cavalry Reserve Corps: Marshal Murat

Total strength approximately: 0 infantry, 5,800 cavalry, 380 artillery and train, 12 guns

1er Heavy Cavalry Division: GD Nansouty

Brigade: GB Piston
1er Carabiniers (3 sqns)
2ème Carabiniers (3 sqns)
Brigade: GB La Houssaye
2ème Cuirassiers (3 sqns)
9ème Cuirassiers (3 sqns)
Brigade: GB Saint-Germain
3ème Cuirassiers (3 sqns)
12ème Cuirassiers (3 sqns)

2ème Heavy Cavalry Division: GD d'Hautpoul

Brigade: Colonel Noirot
  1er Cuirassiers (3 sqns)
  5ème Cuirassiers (3 sqns)
Brigade: GB Saint-Sulpice
  10ème Cuirassiers (3 sqns)
  11ème Cuirassiers (3 sqns)

Light Cavalry Brigade

Brigade: GB Milhaud
  16ème *Chasseurs à cheval* (3 sqns)
  22ème *Chasseurs à cheval* (3 sqns)

Attached to the Cavalry Reserve Corps from I Corps

Light Cavalry Division:

GB Fauconnet

Brigade: GB Treillard
  9ème Hussars (3 sqns)
  10ème Hussars (3 sqns)
Brigade: GB Fauconnet
  13ème *Chasseurs à cheval* (3 sqns)
  21ème *Chasseurs à cheval* (3 sqns)

Artillery Reserve Park

Total strength approximately:
0 infantry, 0 cavalry, 410 artillery and train, 18 guns

The Allied Army at Austerlitz

Supreme Commander: Tsar Alexander
Commander-in-Chief of Allied Forces: General of Infantry Mikhail Kutuzov
Chief of Staff: Generalmajor (GM)

Weyrother
Austrian Commander: Feldmarschalleutant (FML) Prince Liechtenstein
Observing: Emperor Francis I
Overall Commander of First, Second and Third Columns: General Lieutenant (GL) Buxhöwden
Total strength of Austro-Russian Army excluding general staff: 76,410
Approximately 53,035 infantry, 14,450 cavalry, 7,875 artillery and train, 1,050 pioneers, 318 guns (Austrian Army approximately 16,820 men: 11,420 infantry, 3,195 cavalry, 1,775 artillery and train, 430 pioneers, 70 guns); (Russian Army approximately 59,590 men: 41,615 infantry, 11,255 cavalry, 6,100 artillery and train, 620 pioneers, 248 guns)

Imperial Guard: Grand Duke Constantine (Russian Formation)

Total strength approximately: 5,400 infantry, 2,600 cavalry, 980 artillery and train, 100 pioneers, 40 guns

Guard Infantry: GL Maliutin

Brigade: GM Depreradovich I
  Preobrazhensk Guard (2 btns)
  Semeyonovsk Guard (2 btns)
  Izmailovsk Guard (2 btns)
  Guard Jäger (1 btn)
Brigade: GM Lobanov
  Guard Grenadiers (3 btns)
  Guard Pioneers (1 coy)

Guard Cavalry: GL Kologrivov

Brigade: GM Jankovich
  Guard Hussars (5 sqns)

Guard Cossacks (2 sqns)
Brigade: GM Depreradovich II
Chevalier Garde (5 sqns)
Horse Guards (5 sqns)

Army Advance Guard: GL Bagration (Russian Formation)

Total strength approximately:
7,875 infantry, 4,065 cavalry, 735
artillery and train, 0 pioneers, 30
guns (reinforced by two Austrian
batteries at latter stage of battle:
12 guns, approximately 295
personnel)

Brigade: General Maior (GM)
Dolgorukov
5 *Jäger* (3 btns)
Brigade: GM Ulanius
6 *Jäger* (3 btns)
Brigade: GM Kamenski II
Arkhangelogord Musketeer
Regiment (MR) (3 btns)
Brigade: GM Engelhardt
Old Ingermanland MR (3 btns)
Brigade: GM Markov
Pskov Musketeer Regiment
(3 btns)
Brigade: GM Wittgenstein
Pavlograd Hussars (10 sqns)
Mariupol Hussars (10 sqns)
Brigade: GM Voropaitzki
Tsarina Leib-Cuirassier (5 sqns)
Tver Dragoons (5 sqns)
St Petersburg Dragoons (3 sqns)

Attached to Army Advance Guard

Brigade: GM Chaplitz
Khaznenkov Cossacks (5 sqns)
Liselev Cossacks (5 sqns)
Malakhov Cossacks (5 sqns)

Advance Guard of I Column: FML Kienmayer (Austro-Russian Formation)

Total strength approximately:
2,500 infantry, 2,400 cavalry, 300
artillery and train, 250 pioneers,
12 guns
Brigade: GM Carneville (Austrian)
7 *Brod-Grenzregiment* (1 btn)
14 1 *Szeckel-Grenzregiment*
(2 btns)
15 2 *Szeckel-Grenzregiment*
(2 btns)
Brigade: GM Stutterheim (Austrian)
3 O'Reilly-*Chevaulegers* (8 sqns)
1 Merveldt-Uhlanen (1/4 sqn)
Brigade: GM Nostitz (Austrian)
4 Hessen-Homburg-Husaren
(6 sqns)
2 Schwarzenberg-Uhlanen
(½ sqn)
Brigade: GM Moritz Liechtenstein
(Austrian)
11 Szeckel-Husaren (6 sqns)

Attached to Advance Guard

Sysoev Cossacks (5 sqns)
Melentev Cossacks (5 sqns)

First Column: GL Dokhturov (Russian Formation)

Total strength approximately:
7,500 infantry, 250 cavalry, 1,600
artillery and train, 100 pioneers,
64 guns

Brigade: GM Löwis
7 *Jäger* (1 btn)
New Ingermanland Musketeer
Regiment (3 btns)
Brigade: GM Urusov
Yarolslavl Musketeer Regiment
(2 btns)

Vladimir Musketeer Regiment
(3 btns)
Brayansk Musketeer Regiment
(3 btns)
Brigade: GM Liders
Kiev Grenadier Regiment (3 btns)
Moscow Musketeer Regiment
(3 btns)
Vyatka Musketeer Regiment
(3 btns)

Attached to I Column
Denisov Cossacks (5 sqns)

Second Column: GL Langeron (Russian Formation)

Total strength approximately:
10,100 infantry, 360 cavalry, 750
artillery and train, 100 pioneers,
30 guns

Brigade: GM Olsufiev I
8 *Jäger* (2 btns)
Kursk Musketeer Regiment
(3 btns)
Permsk Musketeer Regiment
(3 btns)
Vyborg Musketeer Regiment
(3 btns)
Brigade: GM Kamenski I
Phanagoria GR (3 btns)
Ryazan Musketeer Regiment
(3 btns)

Attached to II Column
St Petersburg Dragoons (2 sqns)
Isayev Cossacks (1 sqn)

Third Column: GL Prshibyshevsky (Russian Formation)

Total strength approximately:

7,560 infantry, 750 infantry and
train, 100 pioneers, 30 guns

Brigade: GM Müller III
7 *Jäger* (2 btns)
Galicia Musketeer Regiment
(3 btns)
Brigade: GM Strik
Butyrsk Musketeer Regiment
(3 btns)
Narva Musketeer Regiment
(3 btns)
Brigade: GM Loshakov
8 *Jäger* (1 btn)
Azov Musketeer Regiment
(3 btns)
Podolsk Musketeer Regiment
(3 btns)

Fourth Column: GL Miloradovich and Feldzeugmeister (FZM) Kollowrath (Austro-Russian Formation)

Total strength approximately: 12,100
infantry (3,180 Russian and 8,920
Austrian), 125 cavalry (Austrian),
1,865 artillery and train, 300
pioneers, 76 guns (40 Austrian and
36 Russian)

Advance Guard: Podpolkovnik (PP) Monakhtin
1 Erzherzog Johann Dragoons
(2 sqns) (Austrian)
Apsheron Musketeer Regiment
(1 btn)
Novgorod Musketeer Regiment
(2 btns)
Brigade: GM Berg
Little Russian Grenadier
Regiment (3 btns)

Novgorod Musketeer Regiment
(1 btn)
Brigade: GM Repninsky
Apsheron Musketeer Regiment
(2 btns)
Smolensk Musketeer Regiment
(3 btns)
Brigade: GM Rottermund (Austrian)
Infantry Regiment 20 Kaunitz
(1 depot btn)
Infantry Regiment 23 Salzburg
(6 btns)
Infantry Regiment 24 Auersperg
(1 depot btn)
Brigade: GM Jurczik (Austrian)
Infantry Regiment 1 Kaiser Franz
(1 depot btn)
Infantry Regiment 9 Czartoryski
(1 depot btn)
Infantry Regiment 29 Lindenau
(1 btn)
Infantry Regiment 38
Württemberg (1 btn)
Infantry Regiment 49 Kerpen
(1 depot btn)
Infantry Regiment Reuss-Greitz
(1 depot btn)
Infantry Regiment Beaulieu
(1 btn)

Fifth Column: FML Johann Liechtenstein (Austro-Russian Formation)

Total strength approximately:
0 infantry, 4,650 cavalry (1,170
Austrian and 3,480 Russian), 600
artillery and train, 0 pioneers, 24 guns
(6 Austrian and 18 Russian)

Austrian Cavalry: FML Hohenlohe
Brigade: GM Weber
1 Kaiser Cuirassiers (8 sqns;
2 detached to Army HQ)

Brigade: GM Caramelli
5 Nassau Cuirassiers (6 sqns)
7 Lothringen Cuirassiers (6 sqns)

Russian Cavalry: GL Essen II
Brigade: GM Penitzki
Grand Duke Constantine *Uhlans*
(10 sqns)
Brigade: GL Uvarov
Elisavetgrad Hussars (10 sqns)
Kharkov Dragoons (5 sqns)
Chernigov Dragoons (5 sqns)

Attached to Fifth Column
Denisov Cossacks (2½ sqns)
Gordeev Cossacks (5 sqns)
Isayev Cossacks (4 sqns)

FURTHER READING

Alombert, P.C. and J. Colin, *La Campagne de 1805 en Allemagne*, 5 vols
  (Paris: Editions Historiques Teissèdre, 2002)
Bowden, Scott, *Napoleon and Austerlitz* (Chicago: Emperor's Press, 1997)
Burton, Lt Col Reginald, *From Boulogne to Austerlitz* (London: G. Allen &
  Co., 1912; reprinted Whitefish, MT: Kessinger Publishing, 2010)
Castle, Ian, *Austerlitz 1805: The Fate of Empires* (Oxford: Osprey
  Publishing, 2002)
Chandler, David, *The Campaigns of Napoleon* (London, Macmillan, 1966;
  reprinted London: Weidenfeld & Nicolson, 1995)
Chandler, David (ed.), *Napoleon's Marshals* (New York: Macmillan, 1987)
Duffy, Christopher, *Austerlitz 1805* (London: Seeley Service & Co., 1977)
Egger, Rainer, *Das Gefecht bei Dürnstein-Loiben 1805* (Vienna:
  Militärhistorische Schriftenreihe, 1986)
———, *Das Gefecht bei Hollabrunn und Schöngrabern* (Vienna:
  Militärhistorische Schriftenreihe, 1982)
Elting, John, *Swords around a Throne* (New York: The Free Press, 1988)
Esposito, Brig Gen Vincent and Col John Elting, *A Military History and
  Atlas of the Napoleonic Wars* (New York: Praeger, 1965; revised
  London: Greenhill, 1999)
Flayhart, William, *Counterpoint to Trafalgar: The Anglo-Russian
  Invasion of Naples, 1805–1806* (Columbia: University of South
  Carolina Press, 1992)
Fremont-Barnes, Gregory (ed.), *Armies of the Napoleonic Wars* (London:
  Pen and Sword, 2011)
——— (ed.), *The Encyclopedia of the French Revolutionary and
  Napoleonic Wars*, 3 vols (Oxford: ABC-CLIO, 2006)
———, *The French Revolutionary Wars* (Oxford: Osprey Publishing, 2001)
———, *The Napoleonic Wars: The Fall of the French Empire, 1813–1815*
  (Oxford: Osprey Publishing, 2002)

Further Reading

————, *The Napoleonic Wars: The Peninsular War, 1808–1814* (Oxford: Osprey Publishing, 2002)

————, *Waterloo 1815* (The History Press, 2013)

Furse, Col George A., *Campaigns of 1805: Ulm, Trafalgar and Austerlitz* (London: Clowes, 1905; reprinted Tyne & Wear: Worley Publications, 1995)

Goetz, Robert, *1805 – Austerlitz: Napoleon and the Destruction of the Third Coalition* (London: Greenhill Books, 2005)

Hollins, David, *Austrian Commanders of the Napoleonic Wars, 1792–1815* (Oxford: Osprey Publishing, 2004)

Horne, Alistair, *How Far From Austerlitz? Napoleon, 1805–1815* (London: Macmillan, 1996)

Hourtoulle, F.G., *Austerlitz: The Empire at its Zenith* (Paris: Histoire and Collections, 2003)

Kagan, Frederick, *The End of the Old Order: Napoleon and Europe, 1801–1805* (New York: De Capo Press, 2007)

Keep, John, *Soldiers of the Tsar: Army and Society in Russia, 1462–1874* (Oxford: Clarendon Press, 1985)

Lachouque, Henry and Anne S.K. Brown, *The Anatomy of Glory: Napoleon and his Guard* (Providence, RI: Brown University Press, 1961; reprinted London: Greenhill. 1997)

Langeron, Alexandre Andrault de, *Journal Inédit de la Campagne de 1805: Austerlitz* (Paris: La Vouivre, 1998)

Lefebvre, Georges, *Napoleon from 18 Brumaire to Tilsit, 1799–1807* (New York: Columbia University Press, 1969)

Lieven, Dominic, *Russia against Napoleon: The True Story of the Campaigns of War and Peace* (London: Penguin, 2011)

Lloyd, Peter, *The French Are Coming! The Invasion Scare, 1803–5* (Tunbridge Wells: Spellmount, 1991)

Macdonnell, A.G., *The March of the Twenty-Six: Napoleon and His Marshals* (London: Prion, 1998)

Manceron, Claude, *Austerlitz: The Story of a Battle* (New York: Norton, 1968)

Mackesy, Piers, *The War in the Mediterranean, 1803–1810* (Cambridge: Harvard University Press, 1957)

Maude, Col Frederick, *The Ulm Campaign 1805* (London: Swan, Sonnenschein, 1912)

Maycock, Capt F.W.O., *The Napoleonic Campaign of 1805* (London: Gale and Polden, 1912)

Mikaberidze, Alexander, *The Russian Officer Corps in the Revolutionary and Napoleonic Wars, 1792–1815* (New York: Savas Beatie, 2005)

Miquel, Pierre, *Austerlitz* (Paris: Michel, 2005)

Palmer, Alan, *Alexander I: Tsar of War and Peace* (London: Weidenfeld & Nicolson, 1974)

Rey, Marie-Pierre, *Alexander I: The Tsar Who Defeated Napoleon* (Chicago: University of Chicago Press, 2012)

Rothenberg, Gunther, *Napoleon's Great Adversaries: The Archduke Charles and the Austrian Army, 1792–1814* (London: Batsford, 1982; reprinted Staplehurst: Spellmount, 1995)

Saul, Norman, *Russia and the Mediterranean, 1797–1807* (Chicago: University of Chicago Press, 1970)

Schneid, Frederick, *Napoleon's Conquest of Europe: The War of the Third Coalition* (Westport, CT: Praeger, 2005)

Schönhals, Karl Freiherr von, *Der Krieg 1805 in Deutschland* (Vienna: Selbstverlag der Redaction der Österreichischen, 1873)

Schroeder, Paul, *The Transformation of European Politics, 1763–1848* (London: Clarendon Press, 1996)

Sherwig, John, *Guineas and Gunpowder: British Foreign Aid in the Wars with France, 1793–1815* (Cambridge, MA: Harvard University Press, 1969)

Smith, Digby, *The Napoleonic Wars Data Book* (London: Greenhill Books, 1987)

Spring, Laurence, *Russian Grenadiers and Infantry, 1799–1815* (Oxford: Osprey Publishing, 2002)

Thiébault, Baron, 'Bataille d'Austerlitz: Passage du Goldbach,' *Spectateur Militaire*, May 1947.

Willbold, Franz, *Napoleons Feldzug um Ulm* (Ulm: Süddeutsche Verlagsgesellschaft, 1987)

INDEX

Austerlitz 1805